T0351065

Mastering React

Mastering React helps the reader master the React JavaScript framework for faster and more robust front-end development.

React is a JavaScript framework for creating interface design that is coherent, cheap, and customizable. It makes it possible to create complicated user interfaces out of "modules," which are small, independent pieces of code. The primary goal of using React is the easier creation of visual interfaces.

React was developed by Facebook and released to the public in 2013. It powers some of the most popular apps, including Facebook and Instagram. It uses virtual DOM (JavaScript Document Object Model), which increases the application's performance. The virtualized DOM in JavaScript is faster than the conventional DOM. React can be used as both a standalone framework and in conjunction with other platforms. It employs component and data patterns to improve clarity while also assisting in maintaining larger applications.

React saves you time and money during development because it is component-based. The design can be segmented into reusable modules that could be used to adjust interfaces dynamically.

The front-end development industry has a reputation for moving at a breakneck speed. Organizations cannot be expected to modify their apps annually to catch pace with technological innovations. This is why businesses prefer React.

React simplifies many things, and its ecosystem is full of valuable sub-frameworks and tools. React is among the most powerful front-end frameworks out there. As such, learning React development can future-proof anyone's career in the long run, and even yield immediate benefits. This book explains the concepts of React in an easy-to-grasp language.

With *Mastering React*, learning React becomes a charm, and readers will undoubtedly advance their careers with the help of this book.

The *Mastering Computer Science* series is edited by Sufyan bin Uzayr, a writer and educator with more than a decade of experience in the computing field.

Mastering Computer Science

Series Editor: Sufyan bin Uzayr

Mastering React: A Beginner's Guide
Mohammad Ammar, Divya Sachdeva, and Rubina Salafey

Mastering React Native: A Beginner's Guide
Lokesh Pancha, Jaskiran Kaur, and Divya Sachdeva

Mastering Ubuntu: A Beginner's Guide
Jaskiran Kaur, Rubina Salafey, and Shahryar Raz

Mastering Visual Studio Code: A Beginner's Guide
Jaskiran Kaur, D Nikitenko, and Mathew Rooney

Mastering Rust: A Beginner's Guide
Divya Sachdeva, Faruq KC, and Aruqqa Khateib

Mastering Bootstrap: A Beginner's Guide
Lokesh Pancha, Divya Sachdeva, and Rubina Salafey

For more information about this series, please visit: https://www.routledge
.com/Mastering-Computer-Science/book-series/MCS

The "Mastering Computer Science" series of books are authored by the Zeba Academy team members, led by Sufyan bin Uzayr.

Zeba Academy is an EdTech venture that develops courses and content for learners primarily in STEM fields, and offers education consulting to Universities and Institutions worldwide. For more info, please visit https://zeba.academy

Mastering React

A Beginner's Guide

Edited by Sufyan bin Uzayr

CRC Press
Taylor & Francis Group
Boca Raton London New York

CRC Press is an imprint of the
Taylor & Francis Group, an **informa** business

First Edition published 2023
by CRC Press
6000 Broken Sound Parkway NW, Suite 300, Boca Raton, FL 33487-2742

and by CRC Press
2 Park Square, Milton Park, Abingdon, Oxon, OX14 4RN

CRC Press is an imprint of Taylor & Francis Group, LLC

Library of Congress Cataloging-in-Publication Data

Names: Bin Uzayr, Sufyan, editor.
Title: Mastering React : a beginner's guide / edited by Sufyan bin Uzayr.
Description: First edition. | Boca Raton : CRC Press, 2023. | Includes bibliographical references and index.
Identifiers: LCCN 2022021394 (print) | LCCN 2022021395 (ebook) | ISBN 9781032313580 (hbk) | ISBN 9781032313559 (pbk) | ISBN 9781003309369 (ebk)
Subjects: LCSH: JavaScript (Computer program language) | Software patterns. | React (Electronic recource)
Classification: LCC QA76.73.J39 M379 2023 (print) | LCC QA76.73.J39 (ebook) | DDC 005.13/267--dc23/eng/20220725
LC record available at https://lccn.loc.gov/2022021394
LC ebook record available at https://lccn.loc.gov/2022021395

ISBN: 9781032313580 (hbk)
ISBN: 9781032313559 (pbk)
ISBN: 9781003309369 (ebk)

DOI: 10.1201/9781003309369

Typeset in Minion
by Deanta Global Publishing Services, Chennai, India

Contents

Mastering Computer Science Series Preface

THE MASTERING COMPUTER SCIENCE covers a wide range of topics, spanning programming languages as well as modern-day technologies and frameworks. The series has a special focus on beginner-level content, and is presented in an easy-to-understand manner, comprising:

- Crystal-clear text, spanning various topics sorted by relevance.

- Special focus on practical exercises, with numerous code samples and programs.

- A guided approach to programming, with step-by-step tutorials for the absolute beginners.

- Keen emphasis on real-world utility of skills, thereby cutting the redundant and seldom-used concepts and focusing instead on industry-prevalent coding paradigm.

- A wide range of references and resources, to help both beginner and intermediate-level developers gain the most out of the books.

The *Mastering Computer Science* series of books start from the core concepts, and then quickly move on to industry-standard coding practices, to help learners gain efficient and crucial skills in as little time as possible. The books assume no prior knowledge of coding, so even the absolute newbie coders can benefit from this series.

The *Mastering Computer Science* series is edited by Sufyan bin Uzayr, a writer and educator with more than a decade of experience in the computing field.

About the Editor

S UFYAN BIN UZAYR IS a writer, coder, and entrepreneur with more than a decade of experience in the industry. He has authored several books in the past, pertaining to a diverse range of topics, ranging from History to Computers/IT.

Sufyan is Director of Parakozm, a multinational IT company specializing in EdTech solutions. He also runs Zeba Academy, an online learning and teaching vertical with a focus on STEM fields.

Sufyan specializes in a wide variety of technologies, such as JavaScript, Dart, WordPress, Drupal, Linux, and Python. He holds multiple degrees, including ones in management, IT, literature, and political science.

Sufyan is a digital nomad, dividing his time between four countries. He has lived and taught in universities and educational institutions around the globe. Sufyan takes a keen interest in technology, politics, literature, history and sports, and in his spare time, he enjoys teaching coding and English to young students.

Learn more at sufyanism.com.

CHAPTER 1

Introduction to React

IN THIS CHAPTER

> ➤ Introduction to React

> ➤ What is React?

> ➤ History of React

> ➤ Advantages and disadvantages

> ➤ Benefits over other JS frameworks

In this chapter, we start with the introduction of React that what is React, and how it can be used for maintaining and designing dynamic web apps. Furthermore, it includes the features and functions provided by it and what its history is, how it came to be developed from the initial to the advanced level. The most important advantages and disadvantages of React and its compatibility with different frameworks of JavaScript are also discussed here.

WHAT IS REACT?

React (also React.js or ReactJS) is the front-end JavaScript library for building user interfaces (UIs) or its components. It is maintained and developed by Facebook (a popular social media platform) and a community of individual developers and companies. It's based in the development pages or applications. However, ReactJS is only concerned with the supervision of states and execution of the states to the DOM, so creating

DOI: 10.1201/9781003309369-1

React applications usually requires the use of additional libraries for routing, as well as certain client-side functionality. In Model View Controller (MVC) architecture, the layer called view layer is accountable for how the app looks like. ReactJS can be easily labeled as a bestseller. Released back in 2013, this JavaScript library has swiftly won popular affection and fame. It is used by most corporations, like Apple, PayPal, and Netflix; more than 32,000 websites are designed and built with the help of ReactJS framework.

Let Us Comprehend This with a Practical Example

Let us consider that one of your friends posted a photograph on Facebook. Now you wanna like the image and so you want to check out the comments beside. Now, when you are browsing over the comments, you see that the likes count has augmented by 100, meanwhile, you liked the picture, even without refreshing the page. This magical count change is due to the use of ReactJS.

React is an indicative, well-organized, and flexible JavaScript library for building user interfaces. It's "V" in MVC.

React1uses a suggestive paradigm that makes it easier to reason about your application and aims to be both effective and supple. It makes modest views for respective states of/your application, and React will resourcefully update and render just the right component when your data varies. The indicative view makes your code more likely and easier to debug.

A React application is done through multiple components, individually accountable for rendering a small, recyclable piece of HTML. Components can be nuzzled within other components to allow multifaceted applications to be built out of simple building wedges. The constituent may also preserve a state – for example, a TabList component may store a mutable corresponding to the present open tab.

Example: Create a new project by using React. Note that all that this component does is render an h1 element containing the name prop. This module doesn't keep the path in a slight state. Here's an ES6 example:

```
import React,{ Component } from 'react';
class App extends Component {
render() {
```

```
        return (
        <div>
                <h1>Hello, Learner </h1>
        </div>
        );
}
}
export default App;
```

Let us consider how it works. At the time of designing client-side applications, a team of Facebook developers observed that the DOM is deliberate. (The Document Object Model (DOM) is an application programming interface (API) for HTML and XML credentials. It defines the logical building of credentials and the way a document is getting into and deployed.) So, to move it faster, React brings in a virtual DOM that is essentially a DOM tree illustration in JavaScript. So, when it is required to read or write to the DOM, it will use its computer-generated illustration. Then the virtual DOM will try to find the most well-organized way to update the browser's DOM.

Unlike browser DOM elements, React elements are simple objects and are economical to create. React DOM mentions updating the DOM to match the React elements. The purpose is to use JavaScript, which is extremely fast and it's worth possessing a DOM hierarchy in it to speed up its manipulation. Although React was perceived to be used in the browser, because of its design, it can also be used along with Node.js.

Why We Should Learn ReactJS?

ReactJS offers elegant resolutions to some of the front-end programming's most tenacious issues. It's fast, scalable, flexible, influential, powerful, and has a strong developer community that's rapidly increasing. You'll grow a strong understanding of React's most crucial concepts: JSX (JavaScript XML), class and function module, props, state, life cycle methods, and hooks (it's been a good feature and must be a powerful concept, it will be discussed later). You'll be able to associate these ideas in React's integrated programming style. I've been exploiting **React** for over a year now. I'm also providing training to assist people to learn React from scratch. I observed that in each training session I was clearing up the same set of notions and concepts over and over. I think those notions are important if you want to "speak React." If you are new to React, this article is very much informative for you as a beginner as we cover each and every point about the library React.

React's admiration today has obscured all other front-end development frameworks. The following are the reasons for this:

- React makes it possible to design dynamic web applications because it does not need as much coding and offers more functionality, contrasting to JavaScript, where coding often gets intricate very swiftly.

- React needs Virtual DOM to operate, thereby creating web applications earlier and faster. Virtual DOM compares the modules' earlier states and apprises only the tuples in the Real DOM that were altered, instead of updating all of the components over and over, as predictable web applications fix.

- Components are the fundamentals of any React app, and a single app typically involves multiple mechanisms. These mechanisms have their logic and controls, and they can be recycled throughout the application, which in turn intensely decreases the application's development period.

- Unidirectional data flow allows a single direction data flow. This means that when developing a React app, developers have to nest child modules within parent components. Because data flows in a single path, it becomes easier to debug faults and pinpoint the location of a problem in an application at the time of questioning.

- The small learning curve made it easy to learn, as it typically combines with basic HTML and JavaScript notions with some valuable accumulation. Still, as in the case with other tools and frameworks, you have to spend some time to get a proper consideration of React's library.

- It is compatible with the development of both web and mobile apps. As we already know React is used for the development of web applications, but that's not all it can do. There is a framework called React Native, resulting from React itself, that is tremendously popular and is used for designing mobile apps. So, it is apparent that React can be used for making both web and mobile apps.

- Facebook has an unconstrained Chrome extension that can be used to debug React apps. This makes debugging React web applications faster and easier.

DOM

The DOM is referred to as the "Document Object Model." In simple words, it's the organized representation of the HTML fundamentals found in a webpage or web app. It represents the entire UI of the application. The DOM is signified as a hierarchy data structure. It contains a node for every UI section present in the web article. It is quite beneficial since it allows the site designer to update the text using JavaScript. The fact that it is in a structured manner also helps a lot because we can quickly pick certain targets and all the code becomes much easier to deal with.

Updating DOM

If you know even a little about JavaScript, you might have realized that people make use of "getElementById()" or "getElementByClass()" classes to the content of DOM. Each time there is an alteration in the state-run of your application, the DOM gets updated to imitate that change in the user interface. As DOM is characterized as a hierarchy itself, updating the hierarchy here is not a costly process indeed we have a much of algorithms on trees to variety the updates reckless. What's demonstrated to be high is that every time the DOM gets updated (rendered), the updated functionality and its base children have to be rendered again to update the user interface of the page. Like this each time there is a module update, the DOM needs to be updated, and the user interface modules have to be re-rendered or updated.

What Are the Foremost Features of React?

Initially we looked at why it is so widespread, now let us figure out the ReactJS features properly. This will help us to clarify how ReactJS performs.

1. **Virtual DOM**: This attribute of React helps to speed up the app development process and offers elasticity. The algorithm simplifies the repetition of a web page in React's computer-generated (virtual) memory.

The original DOM is thereby characterized by a virtual DOM.

Whenever the app is altered or updated, the entire UI is extracted again by the virtual DOM, by updating the modules that have been modified. This decreases the time and cost taken for development.

2. **JavaScript XML or JSX**: It is a markup syntax that defines the attendance of the interface of the application. It creates syntax just like HTML and is used to create React modules by developers.

   JSX is one of the finest features of ReactJS as it is super easy for developers to write the edifice blocks.

3. **React Native**: Uses native rather than web modules to simplify native ReactJS development for Android and iOS. Mostly, this feature transmutes React code to render it compatible with iOS or Android platforms and delivers access to their native characters.

   Uses native rather than web modules to simplify native ReactJS development for Android and iOS. Mostly, this feature transmutes React code to render it compatible with iOS or Android platforms and delivers access to their native characters.

4. **1-Way Data Binding**: This means that React uses a flow of data that is unidirectional, obliging developers to use the call back function to edit modules, avoiding them from editing directly. The monitoring of data flow from a single point is attained with a JS app architecture module called Flux. It really allows developers to better regulate the app and makes it furthermore flexible and effective.

   This means that React uses a flow of data that is unidirectional, obliging developers to use the call back function to edit modules, avoiding them from editing directly. The monitoring of data flow from a single point is attained with a JS app architecture module called Flux. It really allows developers to better regulate the app and makes it furthermore flexible and effective.

5. **Indicative UI**: This means that React uses a flow of data that is unidirectional, obliging developers to use the call back function to edit modules, avoiding them from editing directly. The monitoring of data flow from a single point is attained with a JS app architecture

module called Flux. It really allows developers to better regulate the app and makes it furthermore flexible and effective.

This feature makes React code further comprehensible and easier to fix bugs. ReactJS is the finest platform to develop UIs that are equally thrilling and fetching not just for web apps, but mobile apps as well.

6. **Module-based Manner**: This simply refers that the user interface of an app built on ReactJS is made up of several modules, with each taking its particular logic, written in JavaScript. Due to this, developers can transfer the data across the app without the DOM getting stuck. ReactJS modules play a huge part in determining the app graphics and relations.

This simply refers that the user interface of an app built on ReactJS is made up of several modules, with each taking its particular logic, written in JavaScript. Due to this, developers can transfer the data across the app without the DOM getting stuck. ReactJS modules play a huge part in determining the app graphics and relations.

HISTORY OF REACT: FROM 2010–2017

Back in 2011, the developers at Facebook were facing some problems with code maintenance. As the Facebook Ads application got a cumulative number of features, the team required more people to run immaculately. The growing number of team members and app features reduced them down as a company. Over time, their app became tough to handle, as they required lots of pouring updates. Eventually, engineers at Facebook couldn't keep up with these gushing apprises. Their code necessitated an urgent upgrade to become more effective.

2010: The First Cyphers of React

Xph had been introduced by Facebook into its php stack and it open-sourced it. Xhp is permissible for creating complex components. They introduced this syntax later in React.

2011: An Initial Standard of React

FaxJS has been created by Jordan Walke, the primary model of React; it dispersed an exploration element on Facebook.

2012: Something New Had on Track at Facebook

- Facebook Ads became hard to accomplish, so Facebook needed to come up with good firmness for it. Jordan Walke worked on the prototype and formed React.

- **April 9**: Instagram was acquired by Facebook. Instagram wanted to implement Facebook's new technology. By this, Facebook had a burden to dissociate React from Facebook and make it opensourceable. Most of this was finished by the Facebook developer "Pite_Hunt."

- **Sept. 8–12**: TechCrunch Derange San Francisco, Mark Zuckerberg: "Our huge Mistake Was Betting Too Much On HTML5." He accepted that Facebook would deliver better mobile involvements very soon.

2013: The Year of the Big Inauguration

- **May 29–31**: JS ConferenceUS. Jordan Walke introduced React. React gets open-sourced. Fun Fact: The audience was disbelieving. Most people thought React was an enormous step backward. This happened as mostly "early adopters" joined this consultation, however, React targeted "innovators." The creators of React realized this error on time, and decided to start a "React tour" later on to turn haters into activists.

- **June 2**: ReactJS (by Facebook meta) is available on JSFiddle.

- **July 30**: React and JavaScript XML is available in Ruby on Rails.

- **August 19**: #React and JavaScript XML is available in Python Applications and frameworks.

- **Sept. 14–15**: JSConfEU 2013. #Pete Hunt's speech of rethinking best practices.

- **Dec. 17**: David Nolen Introduces OM, which is based on React. Describes how React is tremendous – which reached early adopters. This object offered how React is recovering more than the other substitutes out there, which boosted the acknowledgment of React.

2014: The Year of Expansion

React had increasingly gained its reputation and is underway to go through to the "early majority" of its latent users. At this point, they needed a new note instead of solely relying on its technical benefits, and it is: how is React stable? By directing on this, they intended to appeal to enterprises, like Netflix.

- **Early 2014**: reactjsworldtour sessions are underway, to build community and to "turn haters into promoters."

- **Jan. 2**: React Developer Tools develops an allowance of the Chrome Developer Tools.

- **February**: Atom was announced – a hackable text editor for the 21st century.

- **April 7–9**: React London 2014.

- **June**: ReactiveX.io emerged.

- **July 13**: The Release of React Hot Loader. React Hot Loader is a plugin that permits React components to be live-reloaded without the loss of state.

- **Dec. 12**: PlanOut: A language for online trials. The proclamation of PlanOut 0.5, which encompasses a React-based PlanOut language editor, and brings the interpreter into feature parity with the new version of PlanOut used internally at Facebook.

2015: React Is Stable

- **Early 2015**: Flipboard issues React Canvas.

- **January**: Netflix likes React.

- **Early 2015**: Airbnb uses React.

- **Jan. 28–29**: React.js Conference 2015 – Facebook released the very first version of React Native for the React.js Conf 2015 through a technical talk.

- **February**: Introduction to Relay and GraphQL at React.js Conference.

- **March 25**: Facebook declared that React Native for iOS is open and available on GitHub.

- **June 2**: Redux launched.

- **Sept. 2**: React Developer Tools, the first stable and original version, is launched.

- **Sept. 14**: React Native for Android was released.

2016: React Gets Mainstream

- **March**: The introduction of Mobx.

- **February 22–23**: React.js Conf 2016, San Francisco.

- **February 22–23**: Draft.js was introduced at React.js Conf 2016 by Isaac Salier-Hellendag.

- **March**: The introduction of React Storybook.

- **June 2–3**: ReactEurope 2016.

- **July 11**: Introducing React's Error Code System.

- **November**: The summary of Blueprint – a React UI toolkit for the web.

2017: The Year of Further Enhancements

- **Early 2017**: A new open-source library named as React Sketch .a pp was introduced by Airbnb.

- **April 19**: React Fiber becomes open-sourced at F8 2017.

- **September**: Relicensing React, Jest, Flow, and Immutable.js.

- **Sept. 26**: #React 16: Error boundaries, portals, fragments, and the Fiber architecture.

- **October**: #Netflix removes client-side React.js.

- **Nov. 28**: #React v16.2.0: Improved support for fragments.

ADVANTAGES AND DISADVANTAGES

ReactJS is the widely used free and open-source JavaScript Library. It let you create impressive web apps that require minimal effort and coding. Its principal objective is to develop UIs that enhance the efficiency of the apps. There are important merits and demerits of ReactJS.

Advantages

1. **Easy to Learn and Use**: ReactJS is really simple to understand and apply. Its documentation, tutorials, and training resources are much easier to understand. Anyone from a JavaScript background can easily get it and start creating web apps using React in a few days. It allows you to get access by just importing the React library and then the function components can directly be used.

2. **Creation of Dynamic Web Applications Becomes Easier**: Making a dynamic web application using HTML strings was problematic because it requires complex coding, whereas ReactJS sorts out that issue and makes it simple. It requires less code and increases the functionality of your product. It includes several concepts that make the website more dynamic. We will consider this in other chapters.

   Making a dynamic web application using HTML strings was problematic because it requires complex coding, whereas ReactJS sorts out that issue and makes it simple. It requires less code and increases the functionality of your product. It includes several concepts that make the website more dynamic. We will consider this in other chapters.

3. **Reusable Components**: A ReactJS web application is a build-up of contrasting components, and every component has its own logic and controls. These components are accountable for getting a small, reusable piece of HTML code that can be further reused wherever you need them. This refillable code makes your apps easier to develop and maintain. It allows you to directly add the functions on your application that gives more attributes to your project.

4. **Performance Enrichment**: ReactJS advances performance due to virtual DOM (Document Object Model). The DOM is a cross-platform and programming API (Application Programming Interface)

that deals with HTML, XML, or XHTML. The main problem arises when DOM was updated, which reduced the performance of the application. Consequently, by introducing virtual DOM, it is present entirely in the memory and is a representation of the web browser's DOM. As we carved a React component, we did not write right to the DOM. As a substitute for writing to virtual components, React will turn into the DOM, leading to smoother and faster performance.

5. **The Sustenance of Handy Tools**: ReactJS has gained popularity due to the availability of a useful collection of tools. These technologies make developers' jobs more rational and easier. The React Developer Tools have been considered as Chrome and Firefox dev extension and allow you to review the React component pyramids in the virtual DOM. It also allows you to select specific mechanisms and examine and edit their present props and state.

6. **Recognized to Be SEO-friendly**: Outdated JavaScript frameworks have an issue in dealing with SEO. The search engines usually have trouble understanding JavaScript-heavy applications. Many web developers have frequently decried this issue. This problem is solved by ReactJS, which allows developers to easily avoid being found on multiple search engines. As a result, React.js apps may execute on the server, with the virtual DOM interpreting and returning a conventional web page to the browser.

7. **The Advantage of Having JavaScript Library**: Currently, ReactJS is picked by most web developers. This is because it is offering a very rich JavaScript library. The JavaScript library affords more flexibility to the web developers to choose the way they need.

In view of ReactJS merits and demerits, it can be effortlessly summed up in three.

8. **Scope for Testing the Codes**: ReactJS applications are tremendously easy to test. It offers a choice where developers can trial and debug their codes with the help of inherent tools.

Arguments: nonrisky, approachable, and progressive. The chief idea behind this precise library is "to design large-scale applications through figures that change frequently again and again"; and it blocks the task well. It provides developers the ability to work with a computer-generated (virtual) browser (DOM) that is much faster and more user-friendly than the actual one. Apart from that, it offers the easier designing of interactive user interfaces, JSX support, component-based construction, and a lot more. These above-mentioned factors make it a realistic prime choice for both start-ups and enterprises.

Disadvantages

1. **The High Leap of Development**: The high leap of development has both benefits and shortcomings. In the event of a disadvantage, because the situation changes so quickly, some engineers are dissatisfied with having to relearn new ways of doing things on a regular basis. They may find it challenging to embrace all of these changes, especially with the regular updates. They must maintain their skills up to date and discover new ways to do things.

2. **Underprivileged Documentation**: It is another demerit which is common in repetitively keeping informed technologies. React technologies are restructured and fast-tracked so fast that there is no time to make appropriate documentation. To overcome this, developers write commands on their own with the evolution of new releases and tools in their current projects.

3. **View Part**: ReactJS maintains and develops only the user interface of applications, nothing else. So you are still required to indicate some other technologies to get a whole tooling set for development in the project.

4. **JSX as a Barrier**: ReactJS uses JSX. It's a syntax extension that is a mixture of HTML as well as JavaScript together. This tactic has its own aids, but some associates of the development community consider JSX as a barricade, exclusively for new developers. Developers grumble about its difficulty in the learning bend.

BENEFITS OVER OTHER JS FRAMEWORKS

A framework is a structural environment for developing dynamic web pages, whereas a framework provides the contrasting features of the development of contrasting components but that are complex to use as for this you must have deep knowledge, whereas React library is much more efficient to use because it is easy to understand and use. Those who are new to the developer line must go to React for creating the most stable project.

Angular or Ember are frameworks (of JS) where some decisions are previously made for you. React is just a library and you require to make all verdicts by yourself. It emphasizes on helping you to build user interfaces with the use of components. ReactJS is a UI library that helps in taking over the scrupulous task in the management of execution of the UI.

- Since it is just a library, you don't need to be opinionated in your coding structure, unlike frameworks.

- With React you can use the latest pure JavaScript since React encourages that, and using Babel you can write future implementations of JavaScript syntax today.

- React has a separate library for handling the DOM (React-DOM), and it's blazing fast since it doesn't directly manipulate the DOM (one of the slowest processes). Instead, it uses a technique called virtual DOM. It chiefly preserves the DOM in JavaScript (which is faster than DOM handling). React compares this virtual DOM with the actual for the most minimal changes required to update the actual DOM and updates accordingly. That's why it is blazing fast.

- React has a huge ecosystem of open-source libraries to choose from that's just incredible for the freedom it gives.

- React uses a component-based approach. Here, every element in the DOM can be a component. This approves the finest coding principles of isolated fragments of code and concepts, which is easier to debug, maintain, and reuse!

Now that you're clear about the compensations and best practices of ReactJS framework, it should come as no wonder that most large and middle-sized companies are leveraging ReactJS development facilities to design their website's user interfaces. So, if you're looking for a ReactJS developer that can completely grasp your needs and provide the greatest results for your ReactJS projects.

CHAPTER 2

Basics of React

JSX (JavaScript XML)

IN THIS CHAPTER

➢ Basics

➢ JSX

➢ Setup

➢ First component props

➢ State methods

In this chapter, we will study what is JSX in React and how to use JSX with React. We recommend using JSX with React. We will also clarify what the user interface (UI) should look like. JSX might remind you of template language, but it is composed with full additional concepts of JavaScript.

For a student who wants to learn front-end development, JSX is the primary choice after HTML, CSS, and JavaScript, a framework that will allow you to create your first project easily.

Most learners begin with ReactJS. The reason is that it is pretty popular and can be easily manipulated with the framework. So, when you are already using Create React App to set up your new assignment, you may realize something supported or something newfangled.

DOI: 10.1201/9781003309369-2

Constituent's files will have an explicit extension, which is not used for non-ReactJS developers, it's |.jsx|. Why not |.js|? What's the definite JSX syntax which is used in ReactJS and in what ways has it improved compared to JS?

That's precisely what I will clarify for you in this chapter. I'm going to show you what JSX is, what it's used for, how to use looping in JSX, and the difference between JSX and HTML.

WHAT IS JSX?

The full form of JSX is "JavaScript XML," and it is a syntax extension to JavaScript based in "ES6," the latest "version" of JavaScript. JSX lets us write HTML in React by transposing HTML into React components, which will help you to create UI more easily for your web applications.

When somebody is working on React code, they may find some suspicious HTML-type* code embedded in the JavaScript. What is this suspicious HTML-type* code, and how does it work within React functions? These short snippets of strange HTML-like* code are not HTML (hypertext markup language), but rather "JavaScript XML," a syntactic extension of JavaScript based on ES6. JSX, or JavaScript XML, is a form of markup that allows you to write HTML in React library by converting HTML tags into React elements (components).

Utilizing JSX lets you write HTML elements in JavaScript, which are then rendered to the DOM (Document Object Model). JSX (JavaScript XML) is a React-precise XML/HTML-type syntax that encompasses ECMAScript to consent XML/HTML-type content to coincide together with JavaScript/React code. The composition is considered to be used by preprocessors (transpilers like Babel) to convert HTML-type content confined in JavaScript documents into typical JavaScript modules that a JavaScript engine can recognize.

Using JSX, you may write brief HTML/XML-like edifices (e.g., DOM-like hierarchy blocks) in identical files as JavaScript code, and Babel will translate these expressions into genuine JavaScript code. As a replacement for putting JavaScript into HTML as mentioned earlier, JSX lets us put HTML into JavaScript.

JSX was formed as a research project at DeNA Co., Ltd., one of the world's major social game providers. Kazuho Oku and Goro Fuji are the main developers (aka GFX).

To use the JSX, you can write the subsequent JSX/JavaScript code:

```
var nav = (
  <ul id="nav">
   <li><a href="#">Home</a></li>
   <li><a href="#">About</a></li>
   <li><a href="#">Clients</a></li>
   <li><a href="#">Contact Us</a></li>
  </ul>
);
```

The # place is the address of the other pages which is needed to be hyperlinked and Babel will convert it into the following components:

```
var nav = React.createElement(
  "ul",
  { id: "nav" },
  React.createElement(
   "li",
   null,
   React.createElement(
    "a",
    {href: "#" },
    "Home"
   )
  ),
  React.createElement(
   "li",
   null,
   React.createElement(
    "a",
    {href: "#" },
    "About"
   )
  ),
  React.createElement(
   "li",
   null,
   React.createElement(
    "a",
    {href: "#" },
    "Clients"
   )
```

```
  ),
  React.createElement(
    "li",
    null,
    React.createElement(
      "a",
      {href: "#" },
      "Contact Us"
    )
  )
);
```

The idea of intercourse HTML and JavaScript in a similar file can be a rather argumentative topic. For now, we ignore any discussion on this. Use it if you find it cooperative. If not, transcribe the React code obligatory to generate React nodes. That's your choice. My opinion is that JSX provides a brief and familiar syntax for a crucial hierarchy structure with characteristics that do not need learning a templating language or leaving JavaScript. Together, these can prove to be win-win when developing large applications.

It should be clear that the JSX is easier to read and write over huge pyramids of JavaScript function calls or object literals (e.g., contrast the two code samples in this section). In addition, the React team finds that JSX is better suitable for designing UIs than an outdated templating method (e.g., Handlebars) solution.

Characteristics of JSX

- There are also some other ways to accomplish the same thing without the use of JSX; however, utilizing JSX makes developing a React application easier.

- JSX allows you to write expressions. Any JS expression or React variable can be used as the expression.

- In addition to the extensive chunk of HTML, we must use parentheses, i.e., ().

- JSX generates React elements.

- JSX adheres to the XML standard.

- JSX syntax expressions are changed into ordinary JavaScript function calls after composing.

- For specifying HTML features, JSX uses camelcase representation. TabIndex in JSX, for example, is identical to tabindex in HTML.

WHY USE JSX IN REACT?

Using JSX while developing React isn't required, but it makes creating React apps easier by allowing you to define the UI in HTML. JSX is a "template language" with the "full power of JavaScript," according to its developers.

Not only are JSX visual aids important when working with JavaScript UI, but using JSX also allows React to display more relevant error messages and warnings for simpler debugging. If your HTML is incorrect or missing a parent element, JSX will give an error, so you can fix it right away.

It is not required to write the React programs in JSX, but it facilitates the creation of React apps by allowing you to define the UI in HTML. According to its developer, JSX is a "template language" that supports the full power of JavaScript.

People do find JSX to be a helpful visual aid when working with the JavaScript interface; utilizing JSX allows React to cope with the more useful error messages and warnings for easier debugging. If there is a syntax error present in HTML or it misses a parent element, JSX will show an error your way so you can immediately make it appropriate.

When coding, one choice is to isolate the logic and markup in separate or different files or documents. React combines them together into a single unit called "components." Using JSX allows us to combine the markup (JSX) and logic (JavaScript), returning an output that is "translated" into JavaScript function calls.

Creating React Nodes Using JSX

As we saw in the previous section, you should be comfortable with utilizing the React.createElement() function to create React nodes. For example, by means of this function, one can design React lumps that characterize both HTML DOM nodes and different HTML DOM nodes. I use this familiar function to form two React nodes in the following section.

```
//: React node, that signifies a definite HTML DOM node
var HTMLLi = React.createElement('li',
            {className:'bar'}, 'foo');
```

```
//: React node, which characterizes a custom HTML DOM
            node
var HTMLCustom = React.createElement('foo-bar',
            {className:'bar'}, 'foo');
```

Having been working with JSX as a substitute (consider that you have Babel setup) of React.createElement() to form these React nodes one just has to substitute React.createElement() function calls through the HTML/XML similar tags, which indicate the HTML you'd like the computer-generated virtual DOM to display. The code displayed above can be written in JSX as follows.

```
//: React node, which signifies a genuine HTML DOM node
var HTMLLi = <li className="bar">foo</li>;
```

```
//: React node, which signifies a custom HTML DOM node
var HTMLCustom = <foo-bar className="bar" >foo</
            foo-bar>;
```

It has been observed that the JSX is not in a JavaScript string format and can just be as if you are formatting it inside of a .html extension document. Numerous times the JSX is transformed back into the React.createElement() functions calls by Babel. The conversion taking place is in the subsequent JSFiddle (i.e., Babel is translating JSX to JavaScript, then React is generating DOM nodes).

If you were to inspect the definite HTML formed in the above JSfiddle, it would be expressed as follows:

```
<body>
  <div id="app1"><li class="bar" data-
                    reactid=".0">foo</li></div>
  <div id="app2"><foo-bar class="bar" data-
        reactid=".1">foo</foo-bar></div>
</body>
```

Creating React nodes with the use of JSX is as easy as designing HTML-like code in your JavaScript documents.

If JavaScript XML tags support the XML self-close syntax, then you can make the choice to leave the closing tag off when no child node is used.

If one passes props/characteristics to native HTML elements that are not in the HTML description, React will not render them to the definite DOM. Yet, if you use a custom element (i.e., not a stand HTML element), then arbitrary/custom features will be furthered to convention elements (e.g., <x-my-component custom-attribute="foo" />).

- The class feature has to be written className

- The for characteristic has to be written htmlFor

- The elegance feature takes an entity of camel-cased style properties

- All appearances are based on camel-cased style (e.g., accept-charset is written as acceptCharset)

- To characterize HTML elements/syntax, one must ensure that the HTML tag must be lower-cased.

Rendering JSX to DOM

The ReactDOM.render() function can also be used to render JSX terminologies to the DOM. Actually, after Babel transmutes the JSX, all it is doing is rendering nodes created by React.createElement(). Yet again, JSX is just an opinion in expression for having to write out the React.createElement() function calls.

In the code example, I am rendering a <li> element and a custom <foo-bar> element to the DOM using JSX expressions.

Once rendered to the DOM, the HTML will look like as follows:

```
<body>
  <div id="app1"><li class="bar" data-
        reactid=".0">foo</li></div>
  <div id="app2"><foo-bar classname="bar"
        children="foo" data-reactid=".1">foo</
        foo-bar></div>
</body>
```

Keep in mind that the JSX in your JavaScript files is taken by the Babel and the Babel transforms the code into React node (i.e., React.createElement() functions calls), and then by means of these nodes forms React (i.e., the Virtual DOM) as a template for generating an authentic HTML DOM subdivision. The part where the React nodes are curved into the actual DOM nodes and further to the DOM in an HTML page ensues when ReactDOM.render() is so-called.

Notes

- Any DOM nodes inside of the DOM element in which you are inter-preting will be removed/substituted.

- ReactDOM.render() does not adjust the DOM component node in which you are translating React.

- Interpretation to an HTML DOM is only one choice with React, other rendering APi are offered. For example, it is also probable to render to a string (i.e., ReactDOMServer.renderToString()) on the server side.

- Re-rendering to the same DOM element will keep informed the existing child nodes if a modification (i.e., diff) has happened or a new child node has to be situated added.

- Do not render this.render() by yourself and leave that it to React.

Using JavaScript Expressions in JSX

Hopefully, by now it is clear that JSX is just a category of syntactical sugar that gets transformed into real JavaScript. But what happens when you want to interact with actual JavaScript code inside JSX? To write a JavaScript appearance within JSX you will have to mention the JavaScript code in { } brackets.

There is a mixing of JavaScript terminologies (e.g., 2+2) in the React/JSX code below, surround by { } among the JSX that will ultimately get assessed by JavaScript.

The JSX conversion will result in the following:

```
var label = '2 + 2';
var inputType = 'input';
var reactNode = React.createElement(
  'label',
  null,
  label,
  ' = ',
  React.create_Element('input', { type: inputType,
                    value: 2 + 2 })
);
```

ReactDOM.render(reactNode, document.getElementById('app1'));

Once this code is analyzed by a JavaScript engine (i.e., a browser), the JavaScript terminologies are evaluated and the subsequent HTML will look like this:

```
<div id="app1">
  <label data-reactid=".0"><span data-reactid=".0.0">2
                + 2</span><span data-
                reactid=".0.1"> = </span><input
                type="input" value="4" data-
                reactid=".0.2"></label>
</div>
```

Nothing very complex is going on here once you comprehend that the brackets basically escape the JSX. The { } brackets purely convey to the JSX that the content is JavaScript and so authorize it alone so it can ultimately be parsed by a JavaScript engine (e.g., 2+2). Note that "{ }" brackets can be used anywhere in the JSX terminologies as long as the consequence is valid JavaScript.

JSX FOR LOOP

When you had wanted to generate a list of JSX elements/components, and you'd like to use a loop for that, it allows you by creating an array of JSX elements/components that could be later shown. Let us have the code example:

```
render() {
        const children = [,John', ,Mark', ,Mary'];
        const childrenList = [];

        for (let [index, value] of children.entries()) {
                childrenList.push(<li
                        key={index}>{value}</li>);
        }


        return <ul>{items}</ul>
}
```

But there is also an alternate solution for doing the same, which is more ReactJS and JSX friendly, it's .map(). Let us consider the code for this method:

```
render() {
        const children = [,John', ,Mark', ,Mary'];

        return (
                <ul>
                        {children.map((value, index) => {
                                return <li key={index}>
                                        {value}</li>
                        }))
                </ul>
        )
}
```
Is it simple and easy, right?

JSX VS. HTML

JSX is popularly used in React, and I will be highlighting the key differences between JSX and HTML syntax. In this section, we are going to compare JSX with HTML. As a front-end developer, you must know that HTML is a Hypertext Markup Language which is used to design the different components that one can see on the screen, like lists, divs, images, etc.

On the other hand, JSX is a form of JavaScript extension that allows designing the HTML elements inside the JavaScript code.

The prime difference between JSX and HTML is that nested JSX must return just one element. It means that if you'd like to create sibling elements, they always need to have parents, but in HTML, this is not necessary.

Let's see the code:

```
// JSX
<div>
        <p>Mary</p>
        <p>Judy</p>
        <p>John</p>
</div>
// HTML
<p>Mary</p>
<p>Judy</p>
<p>John</p>
```

If JSX code wouldn't have a div parent, it couldn't compile, and it would display the error at runtime.

Another difference is that with the HTML we can add a class keyword to define CSS various classes, but with JSX, this keyword has already been taken; that's why the developer had to find out something else. In JSX, we have to mention className to define class names to be used with the styles. It's similar to that property, like onclick in HTML and onClick in JSX.

The succeeding difference is that in JSX any element can be inscribed as a self-ending tag if there aren't any children components inside it. In HTML, there are fewer elements that have self-closing tags; the others have separate opening and closing tags.

Use of className in Its Place of the Class Attribute

In JSX we use the className characteristic while in HTML we use the class feature. This is because JSX is translated into JavaScript and class is a mentioned word in JavaScript.

JSX
```
<div className = "content"></div>
```

HTML
```
<div class = "content"></div>
```

Self-closing tags

Self-closing tags in JSX should have the forward slash, whereas the forward slash is noncompulsory in the HTML self-closing tags.

JSX
```
<img src="abc.html" />
<br/>
```

HTML
```
<img src=" abc.html " >
<br>
```

Event Listeners

Event auditors in JSX are written in camelCase (it's a type of formatting in which the second term word is capital), for instance, onClick, whereas in HTML, they are written in lowercase, for instance, onclick.

Installation or Setup

ReactJS | Setting up the Development Environment

To run the React application, we should have NodeJS installed on our PC. So, the very initial step will be to install NodeJS.

- **Step 1:** for the Installation of NodeJS, one must visit its official download link. Download and install the new version of NodeJS. Once you have set up the NodeJS files on your PC, you need to set up React Boilerplate.

- **Step 2:** If you want to set up React environment for older and latest versions, follow any steps as per your node version.

For older versions that contain "Node < 8.10" and "npm < 5.6": Setting up React Boilerplate, we will install the boilerplate globally. To install the React Boilerplate, enter the following line into your terminal or command prompt:

."npm install -g create-react-app" the command.

Using react-dom.js and react.js in an HTML Page

The react.js file is the main file required to form React fundamentals and write react elements. When you propose to render your elements in an HTML text (i.e., the DOM), you'll similarly require the react-dom.js file. The react-dom.js file is hooked on the react.js file and must be involved together with the react.js file.

An example of an HTML document appropriately including React is as follows:

```
<!DOCTYPE html>
<html>
 <head>
  <script src="https://fb.me/react-15.2.0.js"></script>
  <script src="https://fb.me/react-dom-15.2.0.js"><//
            script>
 </head>
<body>
</body>
</html>
```

By means of the react.js file and react-dom.js file loaded into an HTML page, it is likely to form React nodes/components and then render them to the DOM. The HTML below creates a Hello_Message React module with a React div> node that is rendered to the DOM inside the div id="app">/div> HTML component.

```
<!DOCTYPE html>
<html>
  <head>
    <script src="https://fb.me/react-15.2.0.js"></
             script>
    <script src="https://fb.me/react-dom-15.2.0.js"></
             script>
  </head>
<body>
  <div id="app"></div>
  <script>
    var HelloMessage = React.createClass({
       displayName: 'HelloMessage',
       render: function render() {
        return React.createElement('div',null,'Hello '
                              ,this.props.name);
       }
    });
    ReactDOM.render(React.createElement(HelloMessage,{
       name: 'John' }), document.getElementById('app'));
  </script>
</body>
</html>
```

This setup is all you require to work with React. However, this setup does not allow to work with JSX. There will be a discussion of JSX usage in the next section.

Note: An alternate react.js file termed react-with-addons.js is available, comprising an assortment of utility components for designing of React applications. In place of the react.js document, the "addons" file can be used.

Try not to make the <body> element of the root node for your React app. You should always put a root <div> into <body>, give it an "ID", and render <div> into <body>. This provides React with its own environment to play in without disturbing about what else potentially needs to make variations to the children of the <body> element.

USING JSX VIA BABEL

In the HTML page below, the React HelloMessage constituent and React div> element node were created using the React.createClass() and React. createElement() function methods. This code should look acquainted as it is indistinguishable from the HTML from the previous section. This HTML will run without compilation error in ES5 browsers.

```
<!DOCTYPE html>
<html>
  <head>
    <script src="https://fb.me/react-15.2.0.js"></
                script>
    <script src="https://fb.me/react-dom-15.2.0
                .js"></script>
  </head>
<body>
  <div id="app"></div>
  <script>
    var HelloMessage = React.createClass({
      displayName: 'HelloMessage',
      render: function render() {
        return React.createElement('div',null,'Hello '
                                    ,this.props.name);
      }
    });
    ReactDOM.render(React.createElement(HelloMessage,{
      name: 'John' }), document.getElementById('app'));
  </script>
</body>
</html>
```

Optionally, with the use of JSX via Babel, it is likely to simplify the formation of React components by extracting the React.createElement().

JavaScript function calls so that it can also be written in a more usual HTML like style and syntax.

As a replacement for writing the following, that is React.createElement():

return React.createElement('div',null,'Hello ',this.props.name);

Using JSX, it can be written as follows:

return <div>Hello {this.props.name}</div>;

And after that Babel will translate it back to the code, which uses React. createElement() so it can be analyzed by a JavaScript engine.

It has been specified that you can deliberate JSX as a form of HTML that you can straight away write in JavaScript that needs a conversion step, done by Babel, into ECMAScript 5 code that browsers can smoothly compile and run. In other words, Babel will interpret JSX to React.createElement function calls.

For now, just comprehend that JSX is an elective abstraction providing for your suitability when designing React elements, and it won't run in ES5 browsers without first being transmuted by Babel.

Converting JSX via Babel in the Browser

Generally, Babel default is set up to automatically process your JavaScript files at the time of development with the use of the Babel CLI tool (e.g., via something like webpack). However, it is likely to use Babel straight in the browser by way of a script comprise. And since we are just getting started, we'll avoid CLI tools or learning a component loader in order to study React.

The Babel project inadvertently, as of Babel 6, does not include the script file required (i.e., browser.js) to translate JSX code to ES5 code in the browser. Thus, it is better to use an older version of Babel (i.e., 5.8.23) that offers the needed file (i.e., browser.js) for changing JSX/ES* in the browser.

With the use of browser.js (Babel 5.8.23) to Convert JSX in the Browser

In the HTML file shown below the React code, we have been working to design the HelloMessage module, which is efficient to use JSX. The conversion of the code is stirring for the reason that we have involved the browser .js Babel file and specified the <script> component a type characteristic of type="text/babel".

```
<!DOCTYPE html>
<html>
  <head>
    <script src="https://fb.me/react-15.2.0.js"></
            script>
    <script src="https://fb.me/react-dom-15.2.0
            .js"></script>
    <script src="https://codnjs.cloudflare.com/ajax/
            libs/babel-core/5.8.23/browser.min
            .js"></script>
```

```
    </head>
<body>
  <div id="app"></div>
  <script type="text/babel">
    var HelloMessage = React.createClass({
      render: function() {
        return <div>Hello {this.props.name}</div>;
      }
    });

    ReactDOM.render(<HelloMessage name="John" />,
                  document.getElementById('app'));
  </script>
</body>
</html>
```

Having JSX transmuted in the browser, while appropriate and easy to set up, isn't supreme since the conversion cost is occurring at runtime. Thus, using browser.js has never been a production solution.

Note: The Babel tool is a subjective assortment from the React team for transmuting ES* code and JSX syntax to ES5 code. You can learn more about Babel by reading the Babel handbook.

By Using JSX

Less procedural people can still understand and change the obligatory parts. CSS architects and designers will find JSX more familiar than JavaScript alone.

You can control the complete influence of JavaScript in HTML and avoid using or learning a scripting language. JSX is not a templating solution or answer. JSX is a declarative syntax used to express or display a tree structure of user interface components or modules.

The compiler will search and find errors in your HTML that you might miss while coding.

JSX promotes the idea of inline styles, which can be a good thing.

A JSX specification is presently being written so that it may be used by anybody as an XML-like syntax extension to ECMAScript with no stated semantics.

USING ES6 AND ES* WITH REACT

Babel is not part of React. In fact, Babel's resolve isn't even that of a JSX modifier. Babel is a JavaScript compiling program first. It receives ES* code and converts it to run in browsers that don't sustain ES* code. Today, Babel typically takes ES6 and ES7 codes and converts them into ES5 code. When doing this ECMAScript conversion, it is minor to also alter JSX terminologies into React.createElement() calls. This is what we inspected in the previous section.

Given that Babel is the sequence of steps for transmuting JSX, it makes you write code that will run in forthcoming forms of ES*.

In the HTML page mentioned, the acquainted HelloMessage module has been again written to take benefit of ES6 classes. Not only is Babel transmuting the JSX syntax, it is also transmuting ES6 class syntax to ES5 syntax, which can then be analyzed by ES5 browser engines.

```
<!DOCTYPE html>
<html>
  <head>
    <script src="https://fb.me/react-15.2.0.js"></
script>
    <script src="https://fb.me/react-dom-15.2.0
.js"></script>
    <script src="https://codnjs.cloudflare.com/ajax/
libs/babel-core/5.8.23/browser.min.js"></script>
  </head>
<body>
  <div id="app"></div>
  <script type="text/babel">

    class HelloMessage extends React.Component { //
        notice use of React.Component
      render(){
        return <div>Hello {this.props.name}</div>;
      }
    };

    ReactDOM.render(<HelloMessage name="John" />,
            document.getElementById('app'));

    /*** PREVIOUSLY ***/
```

```
    //* var HelloMessage = React.createClass({
    *     render: function() {
    *         return <div>Hello {this.props.name}</div>;
    *     }
    * });
    *
    * ReactDOM.render(<HelloMessage name="John" />,
document.getElementById('app'));
    */
  </script>
</body>
</html>
```

In the code mention above HTML file Babel is taking in:

```
class HelloMessage involves React.Component {
  render(){
    return <div>Hello {this.props.name}</div>;
  }
};

ReactDOM.render(<HelloMessage name="John" />,
        document.getElementById('app'));
```

and transmuting it to this:

```
"use strict";
var _createClass = (function () { function
    defineProperties(target, props) { for (var i = 0;
    i < props.length; i++) { var descriptor =
    props[i]; descriptor.enumerable = descriptor.
    enumerable || false; descriptor.configurable =
    true; if ("value" in descriptor) descriptor.
    writable = true; Object.defineProperty(target,
    descriptor.key, descriptor); } } return function
    (Constructor, protoProps, staticProps) { if
    (protoProps) defineProperties(Constructor.
    prototype, protoProps); if (staticProps)
    defineProperties(Constructor, staticProps);
    return Constructor; }; })();

var _get = function get(_x, _x2, _x3) { var _again =
    true; _function: while (_again) { var object =
    _x, property = _x2, receiver = _x3; _again =
```

```
false; if (object === null) object = Function.
prototype; var desc = Object.getOwnPropertyDescri
ptor(object, property); if (desc === undefined) {
var parent = Object.getPrototypeOf(object); if
(parent === null) { return undefined; } else { _x
= parent; _x2 = property; _x3 = receiver; _again
= true; desc = parent = undefined; continue _
function; } } else if ("value" in desc) { return
desc.value; } else { var getter = desc.get; if
(getter === undefined) { return undefined; }
return getter.call(receiver); } } };

function _classCallCheck(instance, Constructor) { if
        (!(instance instanceof Constructor)) { throw
        new TypeError("Cannot call a class as a
        function"); } }

function _inherits(subClass, superClass) { if (typeof
        superClass !== "function" && superClass !==
        null) { throw new TypeError("Super
        expression must either be null or a
        function, not " + typeof superClass); }
        subClass.prototype = Object.crea
        te(superClass && superClass.prototype, {
        constructor: { value: subClass, enumerable:
        false, writable: true, configurable: true }
        }); if (superClass) Object.setPrototypeOf ?
        Object.setPrototypeOf(subClass, superClass)
        : subClass.__proto__ = superClass; }

var HelloMessage = (function (_React$Component) {
  _inherits(HelloMessage, _React$Component);

  function HelloMessage() {
    classCallCheck(this, HelloMessage);

    _get(Object.getPrototypeOf(HelloMessage.prototy
      pe), "constructor", this).apply(this, arguments);
  }

  createClass(HelloMessage, [{
    key: "render",
    value: function render() {
```

```
    return React.createElement(
        "div",
        null,
        "Hello ",
        this.props.name
    );
    }
  }]);
  return HelloMessage;
}) (React.Component);
;


ReactDOM.render(React.createElement(HelloMessage, {
    name: "John" }), document.getElementById('app'));
```

Most ES6 features with a few caveats can be used when writing JavaScript that is transformed by Babel 5.8.23 (i.e., https://cdnjs.cloudflare .com/ajax/libs/babel-core/5.8.23/browser.js).

Note: Clearly, one can still use Babel for it is projected to resolve (i.e., compiling newer JavaScript code to older JavaScript code) without using JSX. However, most people using React are taking benefit of Babel for both unsubstantiated ES* features and JSX transmuting.

WRITING REACT WITH JSFIDDLE

The elementary setup that has been defined in this chapter can also be used operational via JSfiddle. JSFiddle uses the identical three resources used in this chapter (react.js, react-dom.js, and browser.js) to make script React online easy and simple.

Below is an embedded JSFiddle comprising the HelloMessage module used in this chapter. On clicking on the "results" tab you can interpret the React module delivered to the DOM. If you have to edit the code, just click on "edit with JSFiddle".

Note that the "Babel" tab designates the JavaScript inscribed into this tab, which will be converted by Babel. Also, the "Resources" tab will show that JSFiddle is dragging in the react-dom.js and react.js files or documents.

It is presumed that after reading this chapter, you will understand the basic requirements to set up React and Babel via browser.js. And that though JSFiddle does not make it apparent, this is the similar precise setup being used by JSFiddle to run React code.

WHAT IS A REACT COMPONENT?

The following section will deliver an intellectual model around the nature of a React module and cover details around forming React components/ elements.

Typically, the only interpretation of a user interface (e.g., the tree or trunk) is divided up into reasonable chunks (e.g., branches). The sapling becomes the starting section (e.g., a layout component) and then each portion in the UI will become a sub-element that can be separated further into sub-components (i.e., sub-branches). This not only keeps the UI prepared but also permits data and state variations to sensibly flow from the tree to twigs, and then sub-twigs.

If this explanation of React module is complex, then I would advise that you inspect any application interface and mentally start isolating the UI into logical lumps. Those chunks possibly are components. React modules are the program of the sequence of concepts (i.e., UI, events/interactions, state changes, DOM changes) making it possible to exactly form these lumps and sub-lumps. For example, a lot of application UIs will have an outline constituent as the top constituent in a UI opinion. This constituent will cover several sub-components, like, maybe, a search constituent or a menu component. The search constituent can then be separated further into sub-components. Maybe the quest input is a distinct component from the button that invokes the search. As you can see, a UI can rapidly convert a tree of components. Today, software program UIs are classically created by making a tree of very simple single accountability components. React offers the means to produce these mechanisms via the "[React.createClass()]" function (or, !@#$React.Component if it uses ES6 classes). The [React.createClass()] function takes in an arrangement entity and yields a React component case.

A React module is mostly any fragment of a user interface that can encompass React nodes (via React.createElement() or JSX). I have consumed a lot of time upfront grooming React nodes so that the elements of a React module would be firmly understood. It seems to be simple till one comes to know that React modules can have other React sub-elements which can result in a composite tree of components. This is not dissimilar to the idea that React nodes can hold other React nodes in a Computer-generated virtual DOM. It might offend your brain, but if you think firmly about it, all a constituent does is wrap itself around a rational set of twigs from a hierarchy of lumps. In this manner, you describe a complete user interface from constituents using React, but the consequence is a tree of React nodes that can easily be interpreted to be somewhat like an HTML text file (i.e., a tree of DOM nodes that forms a user interface).

Creating React Components

A React component that will possibly encompass state can be formed by calling the function called React.createClass().

Example:

```
function Welcome(props) {return <h1>Hello, {props.na
                       me}</h1>;
}

const element = <Welcome name="world" />;ReactDOM
.render(
  element,
  document.getElementById('root')
);
```

This function takes one argument entity used to postulate the specifications of the constituent. The existing constituent confirmation options are mentioned above (a.k.a., component specifications).

render	An essential value, classically a function that yields React nodes, other React components/modules, or null/false
getInitialState	Object comprehending the primary value of this.state
getDefaultProps	Object comprehending standards to be set on this.props
propTypes	Object holding *validation specifications for props*
mixins	Array of mixins (object encompassing approaches) that can *share among components*
statics	Object holding static approaches
displayName	String, identifying the constituent, used in fixing messages. If using JSX this is set by default
componentWillMount	Callback function appealed once directly before the primary rendering happens
componentDidMount	Callback function appealed directly after the primary rendering occurs
componentWillReceiveProps	Callback function appealed when a constituent is getting new props
shouldComponentUpdate	Callback function appealed before rendering when new props or state are being established

componentWillUpdate	Callback function appealed directly before rendering when new props or state are being established
componentDidUpdate	Callback function appealed directly after the component's updates are flushed to the DOM
componentWillUnmount	Callback function appealed directly before a constituent is unmounted from the DOM

The most significant constituent configuration option is render. This conformation option is essential and is a function that returns React nodes and mechanisms. All other constituent configurations are discretionary.

The subsequent code is a sample of generating a Timer React constituent from React nodes using React.createClass().

Make sure you re-cite the remarks in the code.

It appears like a lot of cipher. However, the bulk of the code just involves generating a <Timer/> constituent and then fleeting the createClass() function generating the constituent a formation object containing five properties (getInitialState, tick, componentDidMount, componentWillUnmount, render).

Notice that Timer is capitalized. When generating custom React components you need to capitalize the name of the constituent. Moreover, the value of this among the formation options refers to the constituent illustration fashioned. For now, just contemplate on the conformation options accessible when defining a React constituent and how an orientation to the constituent is attained using keyword "this". Also note that in the code example provided above, I added my own custom instance process (i.e., tick) during the formation of the <Timer/> constituent.

Once a constituent is mounted (i.e., created), you can use the constituent API. The API contains four approaches.

API Method	Example	Description
setState()	this.setState({mykey: 'my new value'}); this.setState(function(previousState, currentProps) { return {myInteger: previousState.myInteger+2}; });	Chief technique used to re-render a constituent and sub-mechanisms
replaceState()	this.replceState({mykey: 'my new value'});	Like setState() but does not combine old state just erases it uses newfangled object sent

| forceUpdate() | this.forceUpdate(function() {callback}); | Calling forceUpdate() will source render() to be called on the constituent, skipping shouldComponentUpdate() |
| isMounted() | this.isMounted() | isMounted() proceeds true if the constituent is rendered into the DOM, false then |

Notes

- The constituent recall conformation options (componentWillUnmount, componentDidUpdate, componentWillUpdate, shouldComponentUpdate, componentWillReceiveProps, componentDidMount, componentWillMount) are also termed as "lifecycle methods" since these numerous methods are performed at precise points in a constituent's life.

- The React.createClass() function is a suitability function that makes constituent illustrations (via JavaScript new keyword) for you.

- The render() method should be a stand-alone function.

That is, it does not modify component state; it produces the same result each time it is used, and it does not read from or write to the DOM or otherwise interact with the browser (e.g., with the use of setTimeout). If you require to interrelate with the browser, accomplish your work in componentDidMount() or the other life span approaches in its place. Keeping render() pure styles server translates into more practical and makes components easier to contemplate about it.

What Are Component Props?

The modest way to clarify component props would be to say that they functionally equal to HTML characteristics. In other words, props provide conformation standards for the component. For instance, in the code below, a Badge component is created and a "name" prop is supplied when the component is initialized.

The name prop is added to <Badge> component in the render method of the <BadgeList> component, where Badge> is utilized, much way an HTML feature is added to an HTML component (i.e., Badge name="Bill" />). After that the name prop is used by the Badge component (i.e., this .props.name) as the manuscript node for the React <div> node condensed by the Badge component. This is like the way how an <input> can take a value feature which it uses to present a value.

The different way to describe about the component props is that they are the configuration values sent to a component. If one considers a non-JSX version of the former code example, it will be apparent that component props are just an object that gets passed to the createElement() function (i.e., React.createElement(Badge, { name: "Bill" })).

```
var Badge = React.createClass({
   displayName: "Badge",

   render: function render() {
     return React.createElement(
       "div",
       null, //no props defined, so null
       this.props.name //use passed this.prop.name as
                         text node
     );
   }
});

var BadgeList = React.createClass({
   displayName: "BadgeList",

   render: function render() {
     return React.createElement(
       "div",
       null,
       React.createElement(Badge, { name: "Bill" }),
       React.createElement(Badge, { name: "Tom" })
     );
   }
});


ReactDOM.render(React.createElement(BadgeList, null),
document.getElementById('app'));
```

This is comparable to in what manner can props be set right on React lumps. Though, when the function createElement() has been passed to a constituent characterization (i.e., Badge) in its place of a node, the props become accessible on the constituent itself (i.e., this.props.name).

Constituent props make it conceivable to re-use the <Badge> constituent with any name.

In the previous set of code example observed in this section, the BadgeList constituent uses two Badge constituents, each with its own this .props model. We can authenticate this by console sorting out the worth of this.props when a Badge constituent is started.

Basically, each and every React constituent illustration has an exclusive illustration property called props that begins as an empty JavaScript entity. The vacant object can get occupied, by a parent constituent, with any JavaScript value/position. These standards are then used by the constituent or conceded on to child components.

Notes

- In ES5 environments/engines, you would not be able to mutate this .props because it's freezing (i.e., Object.isFrozen(this.props) === true;).

- These props should be considered this.props to be read-only.

Sending Component Props

Sending properties to a module entails adding HTML characteristics, like named values, to the constituent when it is used, not when it is definite. For example, the Badge constituent below is described as primary. Then, to send a prop to the Badge module, name="Bill" is added to the constituent when it is used (i.e., when <Badge name="Bill" /> is rendered).

```
var Badge = React.createClass({
  render: function() {
    return <div>{this.props.name}</div>;
  }
});


ReactDOM.render(<Badge name="Bill" />, document.
                        getElementById('app'));
```

Keep in mind that anywhere a constituent is used, a property can be sent to it. For example, the code from the previous section establishes the use of the Badge constituent and name stuff from within the BadgeList constituent.

```
var Badge = React.createClass({
  render: function() {
    return <div>{this.props.name}</div>;
  }
});

var BadgeList = React.createClass({
  render: function() {
    return (<div>
       <Badge name="Bill" />
       <Badge name="Tom" />
    </div>);
  }
});
ReactDOM.render(<BadgeList />, document.
getElementById('app'));
```

Notes

- A component's properties should be considered immutable and modules should not alter within the assets sent to them from above. If you need to modify the belongings of a constituent, then a re-render should occur; don't set props by adding/updating them using this.props.[PROP] = [NEW PROP].

WHAT IS COMPONENT STATE?

Most modules should basically take in props and render. But modules also suggest state, and it is used to supply material about the modules that can be modified over time. Typically, the alteration comes as a consequence of user actions or system actions (i.e., as a response to user input, an attendant appeal or the channel of time).

As per the study on React, documentation state should comprehend data that a section's event handlers may transform to activate a user interface update. In real apps, these data slant to be very minor and JSON-serializable. When structuring a stateful constituent, deliberate about the negligible possible depiction of its state, and only accumulate those possessions in this.state. Inside of render() simply figure out any other info you need to create on this state-run. You'll find that writing apps in this way has a tendency to lead to the most correct application, since accumulation of redundant or figured values to state means that you need to clearly keep them in sync rather than rely on React figuring them for you.

Points that you should keep in mind about React constituent state:

1. If a module has a state, a default state should be provide using getInitialState() function.

2. State transformation is classically how you start the re-rendering of a constituent and all submodules (i.e., children, grandchildren, great grandchildren, etc.).

3. You inform a component of a state transformation by using this.setState() to set an original state.

4. A state transformation combines new data with old data that are already delimited in the state (i.e., this.state).

5. A state changes within deals with job re-renderings. This is something you would never have to do straight render().

6. The state object should only comprise the slight expanse of data needed for the user interface. Don't place figured data, other React constituents or props in the state object.

Working with Component State

Working with a constituent state classically includes setting a constituent default state, accessing the present state, and updating the state.

In the code example below, I am generating a <MoodComponent /> that establishes the use of getInitialState, this.state.[STATE], and this.setState(). If you click on the constituent in a web browser (i.e., the face), it will cycle over the states (i.e., moods) accessible. Thus, the constituent has three possible states, tied to the UI, grounded on clicks by the user interface user. Go forward and click on the express in the consequences tab under.

Note that the <MoodComponent /> has an primary state of ':|', that is set by means of getInitialState: function() {return {mood: ':|'};}, which is used in the constituent when it is first extracted by writing {this.state.mood}.

An occasion auditor is required to alter the state; in this example, a click event on the <span> node that will run the changeMood method. For this purpose, I use this.setState() to cycle to the next vein based on the present mood/state. After the state is apprised (i.e., setState() merges the changes), the constituent will re-render itself and the user interface will alter.

The following points should be kept in mind about React module state:

1. If a module has state, a defaulting state should be provided with the use of getInitialState().

2. State changes are classically how you initiate the re-rendering of a module and all sub-modules (i.e., children, grandchildren, great grandchildren, etc.).

3. The only way a constituent can make its state up-to-date is by using this.setState(). While other ways are likely possible (i.e. forceUpdate()), they must probable not be used (except maybe when mixing with third-party explanations).

4. You inform a constituent of a state transformation by using this.setState() to set a new fangled state. This will result in re-rendering of the module and all children modules that require re-rendering.

5. A state transform combines new data with old data that are previously confined in the state. But this is only a shallow update/merge, it won't do a profound update/merge.

6. A state transformation internally deals with calling re-renders. You should not ever have to call this.render() directly.

7. The state object should only cover the negligible amount of data required for the user interface. Don't place calculated data, other React constituents, or props in the state object.

State vs. Props

A constituent state and props do have some common ground:

1. Both are plain JavaScript objects.

2. Both can have default values.

3. Both can better be accessed/read via this.props or this.state, but neither should be given standards this way. That is, both are read-only when by means of this.

However, both are used for different purposes and in different ways.

Props

1. Props are approved into a constituent from overhead. Either a parent constituent or from the preliminary scope where React is originally rendered.

2. Props are projected as formation values approved into the constituent. Think of them as type arguments passed into a function (if one does not use JSX, that is precisely what they are).

3. Props are absolute to the constituent getting them.

State

1. State is a serializable representation of data component (a JS object) at a point in time that classically is tied to user interface.

2. The component should always start with a default value and then transform the state internally using setState ().

3. The constituent that contains the state, which is sequestered in this intellect, is the only one who can transform it.

4. Don't mutate the state of child constituents. A constituent should never have a collective variable state.

5. State should only comprehend the minimal amount of data needed to characterize your UI's state, it should not comprise figured data, other React apparatuses, or duplicated data from props.

6. State should be circumvented if at all likely. That is, stateless constituents are ideal, stateful apparatuses add complexity. The React documentation proposes: "A common shape is to form numerous stateless constituents that just render data, and have a stateful constituent above them in the order that passes its state to its children via props. The stateful constituent summarizes all of the collaboration logic, while the stateless constituents take care of execution data in an indicative way."

Creating Stateless Function Components

When a module is purely an outcome of props alone, no state, the constituent can be written as a pure purpose evading the need to form a React constituent case. In the example below, code TheComponent is the consequence of a purpose that yields the consequences from React. createElement().

Taking look at the similar code not by means of JSX should simplify what is going on.

```
var TheComponent = function MyComponent(props) {
    return React.createElement(
        "div",
        null,
        "Hello ",
        props.name
    );
};

// ReactDOM.render(React.createElement(MyComponent, {
name: "doug" }), app);
```

Building a React constituent without calling React.createClass() is classically mentioned as a stateless function constituent.

Stateless function elements can't be passed constituent possibilities (i.e., render, componentWillUnmount, etc.). However, .propTypes and .defaultProps can be default set as belongings on the purpose.

The code example below validates a stateless function constituent making use of .propTypes and .defaultProps. You can design as many of your modules as possible, as stateless constituents.

React Components

REACT.COMPONENT

This chapter contains a detailed API reference for the React component class description. It assumes that you're familiar with fundamental React concepts, such as components and props and state and lifecycle. If you are not, read them first in the previous chapter. A component is one of the core structure blocks of ReactJS. In other words, every app you will develop or create in React will be made up of modules called components. Components help to make user interfaces (UIs) much more accessible and more straightforward. You can see UI broken down into several individual pieces called components. Work on them independently and combine them all in a parent/root component which will be your final UI.

React lets you define components as classes or functions. Components described as classes presently provide more attributes, defined in detail later in this chapter. To define a React component class, you have to extend React.Component.

DOI: 10.1201/9781003309369-3

A class component should include the extends React.Component state-ment. This statement creates an inheritance to React.Component, and gives your component access to React.Component's functions.

The component also needs a render() method; this method returns HTML.

Example:

```
import React from 'react';
import ReactDOM from 'react-dom';

function Car() {
 return <h2> welcome to this tutorial!</h2>;
}

function Garage() {
 return (
  <>
        <h1>React Component?</h1>
        <Car />
  </>
 );
}
```

ReactDOM.render(<Garage />, document.getElementById('root')).

This is the only method you must define in React.Component; its sub-class is called render(). All the other methods defined in this chapter are optional.

We strongly recommend against creating or designing your base component classes. In React components, code reuse is mainly achieved through constituting rather than inheritance.

Note: ReactJS does not force you to use the ES6 class syntax. If you pre-fer not to use it, you may use the create-react-class module or a similar custom abstraction instead.

THE COMPONENT LIFECYCLE

Every component has several "lifecycle methods" that you can overwrite to run codes at particular times. You can use this lifecycle illustration as a cheat sheet. In the below list, commonly used lifecycle methods are marked. The rest of them exist for relatively rare used cases.

Mounting

When a component instance is generated and put into the DOM, the following methods and concepts are called in the following manner:

```
constructor()
static getDerivedStateFromProps()
render()
componentDidMount()
```

Note: These methods are considered bequest and you should evade them in new codes:
```
UNSAFE_componentWillMount()
```

Updating

An update can be triggered by changes to props or state. These approaches are called in the following order when a component is being re-rendered:

```
static getDerivedStateFromProps()
shouldComponentUpdate()
render()
getSnapshotBeforeUpdate()
componentDidUpdate()
UNSAFE_componentWillUpdate()
UNSAFE_componentWillReceiveProps()
```

Unmounting

This method has been called when a component is being detached from the DOM:

```
componentWillUnmount()
Error Handling
```

These methods have been called when an error exists during rendering, in a lifecycle process, or in the constructor of any child component.

```
static getDerivedStateFromError()
componentDidCatch()
Other APIs
```

Each component also provides several other APIs:

- setState(),
- forceUpdate(),
- Class Properties,
- defaultProps,
- displayName
- Instance Properties
- props
- state
- Reference

The concepts in this section cover the vast majority of use cases you will encounter designing React components.

```
render()
render()
```

The render() method is the only essential concept in the class component.

When to call, it should examine or demonstrate this.props and this.state and return one of the following types.

React Elements

Typically formed via JSX. For example, <div /> and <MyComponent /> are the React elements that instruct React to render a DOM node, or the other user-defined components, respectively.

Arrays and Fragments

They let you return the multiple elements from render.

- **Portals**: They let you render the children into a different DOM sub-tree.

- **String and numbers**: These are rendered as the text nodes in the DOM.

- **Booleans or null**: Render nothing. (Mostly exists to support the return test && <Child /> pattern, where the test is in boolean.)

The render() method should be pure, which means it should not affect component states, should provide the same output each time it is called, and must not interact directly with the browser.

If you need to communicate with the browser, use componentDid-Mount() or one of the various lifecycle methods. Keeping render() pure makes the components easier to think about.

Note: render() will not be called on if shouldComponentUpdate() returns the false value.

render() will not be called on if shouldComponentUpdate() returns the false value.

```
constructor()
constructor(props).
```

If you do not initialize state and you do not bind methods, you do not need to implement a constructor for your React components.

A React component's constructor is called before it is mounted. You should call super(props) before the other instructions when constructing the constructor for the React.Component subclass. Otherwise, this.props will be un undefined in constructors, resulting in issues.

Typically, React constructors are used only for two purposes:

1. Initializing the local state by assigning the object to this.state.

2. Binding event handler concepts to the instance.

You should not call setState() in constructor(). If your component needs to use local state, assign the initial state to this.state directly in constructor:

```
constructor(props) {
  super(props);
  // Don not call this.setState() here!
  this.state = { counter: 0 };
  this.handleClick = this.handleClick.bind(this);
}
```

Only in the constructor may you explicitly assign this.state. This must be used in all other procedures. Instead use setState().

In the constructor, a void introduces side effects or subscriptions. In certain circumstances, use componentDidMount() instead.

Note: Avoid copying props into state! This is a basic mistake:

```
constructor(props) {
super(props);
// Do not do this!
this.state = { color: props.color };
}
```

The problem is that it is both unnecessary (you can use this.props.color directly instead), and forms an error (updates to the color prop would not reflect in the state).

Use these patterns only if you want to disregard prop modifications, in which case renaming the prop to initialColor or defaultColor makes sense. When necessary, you may force the component to "reset" its internal state by changing its key.

```
componentDidMount()
componentDidMount()
```

componentDidMount() is called on immediately after the component is mounted (inserted into the paradigm). Initialization that needs DOM nodes should go here. If you need to load data from the remote endpoint, this is a good place to instantiate the network request.

This technique is a good place to set up any subscriptions, and if you do that, do not forget to unsubscribe in componentWillUnmount().

You may call setState() instantly in componentDidMount(), and it will trigger an extra rendering. Still, it will render before the browser updates the screen, and this guarantees that even though the render() will be called two times in this case, the user would not see the intermediate states. Use with care because it repeatedly creates performance concerns, and in most circumstances, you should be able to assign the starting state in the constructor() instead. However, it may be essential in scenarios such as modals and tool-tips when you need to measure a DOM node before producing something that is dependent on its size or location.

```
componentDidUpdate()
componentDidUpdate(prevProps, prevState, snapshot)
```

componentDidUpdate() is called on immediately after updating occurs. This concept is not called for an initial render.

Use this as the opportunity to operate on the DOM when the components have been updated, and this is also a good place to do network requests as long as you compare the current props to former props (e.g., a network request may not be necessary if the props have not been changed).

```
componentDidUpdate (prevProps) {
  // Typical usage (do not forget to compares props):
  if (this.props.userID !== prevProps.userID) {
      this.fetchData(this.props.userID);
  }
}
```

You may call setState() directly in componentDidUpdate(), but it must be wrapped in a condition, as seen above, or you will have an infinite loop. It would also result in an additional re-rendering, which, while not apparent to users, might have an impact on the performance of the components. If you are trying to "mirror" some state to a prop coming from above, consider using the prop directly in its place. Read more about the reason copying props into state causes errors.

If your components implement the getSnapshotBeforeUpdate() lifecycle (which is rare), the value it returns will be passed as the third "snapshot" parameter to componentDidUpdate(). Otherwise, this parameter will be undefined.

Note: componentDidUpdate() will not be called if the shouldComponentUpdate() components returns false.

```
componentWillUnmount ()
componentWillUnmount ()
```

componentWillUnmount() is called on instantly before a component is unmounted and destroyed. Perform any important cleanup in this method, such as invalidating timers, canceling network requests, or cleaning up any of the subscriptions formed in componentDidMount().

Because the components will never be re-rendered, you should not use setState() in componentWillUnmount(). Once a components instance is unmounted, it will never be mounted again.

RARELY USED LIFECYCLE METHODS

The approaches in this section resemble uncommon use cases. They are handy once in a while, but most of your components probably do not need them. If you tick the "Show less frequent lifecycles" button at the top of this lifecycle figure, you'll see most of the ways below.

```
shouldComponentUpdate()
shouldComponentUpdate(nextProps, nextState)
```

Use shouldComponentUpdate() to let React know if a component's output is not altered by the existing change in state or prop. The default performance is to re-render on every state's change, and in the vast majority of cases, you should trust the default performance.

shouldComponentUpdate() is summoned before rendering when new props or states are being established. Defaults to true. This technique is not called for the primary render or when forceUpdate() is executed.

This technique only exists as a performance optimization. Don't rely on it to "prevent" an execution, as this can lead to errors. Deliberately use the built-in PureComponent in place of writing shouldComponentUpdate() by hand. PureComponent accomplishes a shallow comparison of props and states, and reduces the coincidental that you will skip an essential update.

You can compare this if you are certain you need to write it by hand: props in conjunction with nextProps and this to indicate that the React update can be ignored, replace state with nextState and return false. Note that returning false values does not stop child components from re-rendering when their state alters.

We do not recommend doing deep equivalence checks or using JSON. stringify() in shouldComponentUpdate(). It is very ineffective and will harm the presentation.

Presently, if shouldComponentUpdate() returns false, then UNSAFE_ componentWillUpdate(), render(), and componentDidUpdate() will not be appealed. ShouldComponentUpdate() may be viewed as a suggestion rather than a strict directive in the years ahead, and providing false may still result in the constituent being re-rendered.

```
static getDerivedStateFromProps()
static getDerivedStateFromProps(props, state)
```

getDerivedStateFromProps is appealed right before calling the render process, both on the initial mount and on consequent updates. It should return the object to update the states or null to update nothing.

This process exists for rare use cases where the state depends on changes in props over time. For example, it might be handy for applying a <Transition> component that equalizes its preceding and subsequent children to confirm which of them to animate in and out.

Deriving states leads to verbose codes and makes your components hard to think about. Make sure you are familiar with simpler alternatives.

If you need to perform the side effect (for example, data fetching or an animation) in response to a variation in props, use componentDidUpdate lifecycle instead.

If you want to re-compute some information only when a prop modifies, use a memoization helper.

If you want to "reset" some states when prop changes, consider either making a component fully precise or entirely abandoned with a key instead.

This process doesn't have access to the component illustration. If you want, you can reuse some code among getDerivedStateFromProps() and the other class methods by removing pure functions of the component props and states outside the class description.

This approach fires on every render, regardless of the cause, as opposed to UNSAFE componentWillReceiveProps, which fires only when the parent causes a re-render and not as a consequence of a local setState.

```
getSnapshotBeforeUpdate()
getSnapshotBeforeUpdate(prevProps, prevState)
```

getSnapshotBeforeUpdate() is appealed right before the most freshly rendered output is committed to, e.g., the DOM. It allows your component to capture some data from the DOM (e.g., scroll position) before it is potentially altered. Any value returned by this lifecycle process will be passed as a parameter to componentDidUpdate().

This use case is not mutual, but it may occur in user interfaces like a chat thread that must handle scroll position specifically.

A snapshot value (or null value) should return.

Example:
```
class ScrollingList extends React.Component {
  constructor(props) {
   super(props);
   this.listRef = React.createRef();
  }
```

```
getSnapshotBeforeUpdate(prevProps, prevState) {
  // Are we adding the new items in a list?
  // Capture the scroll the position so we can adjust
it scroll by further.
  if (prevProps.list1.length < this.props.list1.length) {
    const list1 = this.listRef.current;
    return list1.scrollHeight - list.scrollTop;
  }
  return null;
}

componentDidUpdate(prevProps, prevStates, snapshot) {
  // If do have the snapshot value, we have just
          added the new items.
  // Adjust scroll so these new items do not push the
          old ones out of views.
  // (snapshot here is the value returned from the
          getSnapshotBeforeUpdate)
  if (snapshot !== null) {
    const list = this.listRef.current;
    list.scrollTop = list.scrollHeight - snapshot;
  }
}
render() {
  return (
    <div ref={this.listRef}>{/* ...contents... */}</
                        div>
  );
}
}
```

In the above examples, it is significant to read the scrollHeight features in getSnapshotBeforeUpdate for the reason that there may be delays between the "render" phase lifecycles (like render) and "commit" segment lifecycles (like getSnapshotBeforeUpdate and componentDidUpdate).

ERROR BOUNDARIES

Error limits are React components or modules that catch JavaScript errors from anywhere in their child component model, log those faults, and display the fallback user interface instead of the component paradigm that crashed. Error boundaries catch errors during rendering, lifecycle approaches, and constructors of the whole paradigm below them.

A class component becomes an error boundary that it defines either (or both) of the lifecycle concepts static getDerivedStateFromError() or componentDidCatch(). Updating the state from these lifecycles allows you to capture an unhandled JavaScript error in the below hierarchy and display a fallback user interface.

Utilize error boundaries just to recover from unanticipated exceptions; do not attempt to use them for control flow.

Note: Error boundaries only notice mistakes in the components in the tree below them. An error border cannot capture an error that has occurred within itself.

```
static getDerivedStateFromError()
static getDerivedStateFromError(error)
```

This lifecycle has been invoked after a descendant component has thrown an error. It receives the errors thrown as a parameter and should return the value to the update state.

```
class ErrorBoundary extends React.Component {
  constructor(props) {
    super(props);
    this.state = { hasError: false };
  }

  static getDerivedStateFromError(error) {
    // Update the state so the next render will show the
            fallback User Interface.
    return { hasError: true };
  }

  render() {
    if (this.state.hasError) {
      // You can render any custom fallback UI
      return <h1>Something went wrong.</h1>;
    }

    return this.props.children;
  }
}
```

Note: getDerivedStateFromError() is called at the "render" phase, so side effects aren't permitted. For those cases you must use componentDid-Catch() in its place.

```
componentDidCatch()
componentDidCatch(error, info)
```

This lifecycle has invoked after a descendant component has thrown an error. It receives two parameters:

1. **error**: The error that was thrown.

2. **info**: An object with the componentStack key containing data about which component threw the error.

componentDidCatch() is called at the "commit" phase, so side effects are allowed. It should be used for things like logging the errors.

```
class ErrorBoundary extends React.Component {
  constructor(props) {
    super(props);
    this.state = { hasError: false };
  }

  static getDerivedStateFromError(error) {
    // Update state so that the next render will show
the fallback UI.
    return { hasError: true };
  }


  componentDidCatch(error, info) {
    // Example "componentStack":
    //   in ComponentThatThrows (created by App)
    //   in ErrorBoundary (created by App)
    //   in div (created by App)
    //   in App
    logComponentStackToMyService(info.componentStack);
  }

  render() {
    if (this.state.hasError) {
      // You can render any custom fallback UI
```

```
      return <h1>Something went wrong.</h1>;
    }

    return this.props.children;
  }
}
```

Production and development builds of React moderately differ in the way componentDidCatch() handles the errors.

On development, the errors will be bubbled up to window, this refers that any window.onerror or window.addEventListener ('error', callback) will seize the errors that have been caught by the componentDidCatch().

On production, in spite of the errors it will not bubble up, which means any ancestor error handler will only take errors not clearly caught by the componentDidCatch().

Note: In the event of any error, you can render a fallback user interface with componentDidCatch() by calling setState, but this will be criticized in a future release. Use static getDerivedStateFromError() to handle the fallback rendering instead.

LEGACY LIFECYCLE METHODS

The following lifecycle approaches are marked as "legacy." They still work, but we do not commend using them in the new codes.

```
UNSAFE_componentWillMount()
UNSAFE_componentWillMount()
```

Note: This lifetime was previously known as the componentWillMount lifecycle. That name will be valid until version 17. To automatically update the modules, use the rename-unsafe-lifecycles codemod.

UNSAFE_componentWillMount() has raised just before mounting occurs. It is called before the render(), therefore calling setState() synchronously in this technique will not trigger the extra interpretation. We endorse using the constructor() instead of preparing the states.

You should not introduce any side effects or subscriptions in this technique. For those use cases, use componentDidMount() in its place.

This is the only lifecycle technique called on Server rendering.

```
UNSAFE_componentWillReceiveProps()
UNSAFE_componentWillReceiveProps(nextProps)
```

Note: This lifecycle was formerly called as componentWillReceive-Props, and the term will remain to work until version 17 has been released. Use the rename-unsafe-lifecycles codemod to automatically update your component.

If you need to perform the side effect (for example, data fetching or an animation) in response to the change in props, use componentDidUpdate lifecycle in its place.

Use a memoization helper if you use the componentWillReceiveProps to re-compute some data only when the prop changes.

Instead of utilizing the componentWillReceiveProps to "reset" some state when a prop changes, consider making the component wholly controlled or completely uncontrolled using a key.

UNSAFE_componentWillReceiveProps() is stopped before a mounted component receives a new prop. You can compare this if you need to update the state in response to prop changes: props and nextProps, and use this to make state transitions. In this notion, setState() is used.

Note that if the parent component causes your components to re-render, this method will be called even if props have not been changed. Make sure to differentiate the current and next values if you only want to handle the changes.

React does not call UNSAFE_componentWillReceiveProps() with starting props during mounting. It only calls this concept if some of the component's props may update or modify. Calling this.setState() generally does not trigger UNSAFE_componentWillReceiveProps().

```
UNSAFE_componentWillUpdate()
UNSAFE_componentWillUpdate(nextProps, nextState)
```

Note: This lifetime was formerly known as componentWillUpdate. That name will continue to be valid until version 17 is released. Use the rename-unsafe-lifecycles codemod to update the components automatically.

UNSAFE_componentWillUpdate() is stopped just before rendering when new props or states are acquired. Take advantage of this opportunity to prepare before any upgrade happens. For the initial render, this procedure is not invoked.

Remember that you cannot call this.setState() here; nor should you do anything else (e.g., dispatch a Redux action) that would set up an update to the React component before the UNSAFE_componentWillUpdate() returns.

Typically, this method can be replaced by the componentDidUpdate(). If someone reads from the DOM in this method (e.g., to save a scroll position), one will move that logic to the getSnapshotBeforeUpdate().

Note: Must remember that UNSAFE_componentWillUpdate() will not be invoked if shouldComponentUpdate() returns false(0).

OTHER APIS

Unlike the above lifecycle methods (which React calls for you), the methods below are the techniques you can call from your components.

There are just two of them: setState() and forceUpdate().

```
setState()
setState(updater, [callback])
```

setState() enqueues changes to the component states and tells React that this component and its children require to be re-rendered with the updated states. This is the basic method you use to update the UI in response to event handlers and server responses.

Think of setState() as an appeal rather than an immediate instruction to update the components. React may delay it for better-perceived performance and then update several components in a single pass. React does not guarantee that the state changes are applied immediately.

setState() does not ever immediately update the component. It may batch or defer the update later. This makes reading this.state right next calling setState() a potential pitfall. In place of it, use componentDidUpdate or a setState callback (setState(updater, callback)), either of which is guaranteed to eject after the update has been applied. If you need to set the state based on the former state, read about the updater argument mentioned below.

setState() will all the time lead to a re-render unless shouldComponentUpdate() returns the false value. If variable objects are being used and conditional rendering logic cannot be executed in shouldComponentUpdate(), calling setState() only when the updated state differs from the former state will avoid unnecessary re-renders.

The first argument is an updater or modifier function with the signature.

(state, props) => stateChange

The state is a reference to the constituent state when the changes have been functional. It should not be a straight variable. Instead, changes should be characterized by constructing a new object based on the input from the state and props. For instance, suppose we wanted to increase values in the state by props.step:

```
this.setState((state, props) => {
  return {counter: state.counter + props.step};
});
```

The state and props returned by the updater function are always up to date. The updater's output is mixed with the state on the surface.

The second parameter to setState() is an elective callback function that will perform once setState is accomplished, and the constituent is re-rendered. Normally we recommend using componentDidUpdate() for such logic instead.

You may optionally pass the object as the first argument to setState() instead of a function:

```
setState(stateChange[, callback])
```

This executes a shallow merge of stateChange into the new state, e.g., to correct a shopping cart item quantity:

```
this.setState({quantity: 23})
```

The form of setState() is also asynchronous, and numerous calls during the same cycle may batch-compose. For example, if your effort to increment an item quantity more than once in the identical cycle, that will result in the corresponding of:

```
Object.assign(
  previousState,
  {quantity: state.quantity + 1},
  {quantity: state.quantity + 1},
  ...
)
```

Succeeding calls will override values from prior calls in the same cycle, so the quantity will increment only once. If the next state hinges on the current state, we endorse using the updater function to form instead:

```
this.setState((state) => {
 return {quantity: state.quantity + 1};
});
```

For more detail, see State and Lifecycle Guide.

- **In depth**: When and why is setState() calls batched?

- **In depth**: Why is not this.state updated instantly?

```
forceUpdate()
component.forceUpdate(callback)
```

By default, when your component's states or props are modified, your component will re-render. If your render() technique depends on some other data, you can tell React that the component requires re-rendering by calling forceUpdate().

Calling forceUpdate() will cause render() to be call on component, skipping shouldComponentUpdate(). This will trigger the usual lifecycle approaches for child components and the shouldComponentUpdate() process of each child, and React will still only update the DOM if the markup changes.

Generally, you should try to neglect all uses of forceUpdate() and only read from this.props and this.state in render().

CLASS PROPERTIES

defaultProps

defaultProps can be defined as a feature on the component class itself, to set the default props for class. This is used for the undefined props, but not for null props. For example:

```
class CustomButton extends React.Component {
 // ...
}

CustomButton.defaultProps = {
 color: 'blue'
};
```

If props.color is not provided, it has been set "blue" by default:

```
render() {
  return <CustomButton /> ; // props.color will be
                              set it to blue
}
```

If props.color is set to null that will remain set to null:

```
displayName
  render() {
    return <CustomButton color={null} /> ; // props.col
                            or will remain null
}
```

The displayName string is used for debugging messages. Typically, you do not require to set it explicitly since it is inferred from the name of the functions or classes that describe the components. You might want to set it evidently if we want to display a different name for the debugging tenacities or when we form a higher-order component; see Wrap the Display Name for Easily Debugging for details.

INSTANCE PROPERTIES

Props

this.props holds the props that were clear by the caller of this component. See components and props for an overview of props.

In particular, this.props.children is an exclusive prop, typically clear by the child tags in the JSX appearance rather than in the tag itself.

State

The state encompasses data specific to this component that may alter over time and the state is user-defined, and it should be the plain JavaScript object.

If some value is not used for rendering or data flow (for example, a timer ID), you do not have to put it in a state, and such values can be defined as fields on the component illustration.

Do not mutate this.state directly, as calling setState() afterward may replace the change you made and treat this.state as if it were immutable.

Conditional Rendering

In React, you can generate distinct components that encapsulate your need's performance. Then, you can extract only some of them, depending on the state of your apps.

Conditional rendering in React is similar to how conditions work in JavaScript in that it uses JavaScript operators such as if and the conditional operator to generate elements that represent the current state and then allows React to update the UI to match them.

Let us consider these two components:

```
function UserGreeting(props) {
 return <h1>Welcome </h1>;
}
```

```
turn <h1>Please sign up.</h1>;
}function GuestGreeting(props) {
 re
```

We will create a Greeting component that displays either of these components depending on whether a user is logged in or not:

```
function Greeting(props) {
 const isLoggedIn = props.isLoggedIn;
 if (isLoggedIn) {
  return <UserGreeting />;
 }
 return <GuestGreeting />;
}
```

```
ReactDOM.render(
 // Try changing to isLoggedIn={true}:
 <Greeting isLoggedIn={false} />,
 document.getElementById('root')
);
```

Try it on the CodePen platform.

The given example renders a different greeting depending on the value of the isLoggedIn prop.

ELEMENT VARIABLES

You can use variables to store elements. This can help you tentatively render a part of the component while the rest of the output does not change.

Consider there are the two new components representing Logout and Login buttons:

```
function LoginButton(props) {
 return (
  <button onClick={props.onClick}>
  Login
  </button>
 );
}

function LogoutButton(props) {
 return (
  <button onClick={props.onClick}>
  Logout
  </button>
 );
}
```

In the below example, we will form a stateful constituent called LoginControl.

It will render either <LoginButton /> or <LogoutButton />, depending upon its existing state. It will also render the <Greeting /> from the former example:

```
class LoginControl extends React.Component {
 constructor(props) {
  super(props);
  this.handleLoginClick = this.handleLoginClick.b
ind(this);
  this.handleLogoutClick = this.handleLogoutClick.b
ind(this);
  this.state = {isLoggedIn: false};
 }

 handleLoginClick() {
  this.setState({isLoggedIn: true});
 }
```

```
handleLogoutClick() {
  this.setState({isLoggedIn: false});
}

render() {
  const isLoggedIn = this.state.isLoggedIn;
  let button;
  if (isLoggedIn) {
    button = <LogoutButton onClick={this.
                          handleLogoutClick} />;
  } else {
    button = <LoginButton onClick={this.
handleLoginClick} />;
  }

  return (
   <div>
    <Greeting isLoggedIn={isLoggedIn} />
    {button}
   </div>
  );
 }
}

ReactDOM.render(
 <LoginControl />,
 document.getElementById('root')
);
```

While confirming a variable and using an if statement is an excellent technique to render a component temporarily, there are situations when you may wish to utilize a simpler syntax. There are several ways to inline conditions in JSX, which are discussed here.

INLINE IF WITH LOGICAL && OPERATOR

You might embed expressions in JSX by wrapping them in curly braces. This includes the JavaScript logical && operator. It can be handy conditionally together with an element:

```
function Mailbox(props) {
  const unreadMessages = props.unreadMessages;
  return (
```

```
<div>
  <h1>Hello student !</h1>
  {unreadMessages.length > 0 &&
    <h2>
      You have {unreadMessages.length} unread messages.
    </h2>
  }
</div>
);
}

const messages = ['React', 'Re: React', 'Re:Re:
React'];
ReactDOM.render(
  <Mailbox unreadMessages={messages} />,
  document.getElementById('root')
);
```

It works because in JavaScript, true && expression ever assesses to expression, and false && expression always appraises to false.

Therefore, if that condition is true, the element right after && will appear in the output or result. If it is false, React will avoid and skip it.

WHAT ARE STYLED COMPONENTS

Styled components are the library built for React and React Native developers or creators. They let you use component-level styles in your apps. *Styled components* control a mixture of JavaScript and CSS using CSS-in-JS.

Styled components are based on tagged template literals, meaning actual CSS code is written between backticks when styling your components. This gives developers the flexibility of reprocessing their CSS code from one project to the other.

There is no requirement to map your formed components to external CSS styles with styled components.

Advantages of Using Styled Components

Some of the benefits of employing styled components are as follows:

- **Eliminates class name errors**: Styled components give unique class names for your styles, eliminating the difficulties associated with class name replication, misspellings, and overlaps.

- **Easier managing of CSS**: Because each piece of style is linked to a specific component, it is easy to determine which CSS is being used. This makes it simple to get rid of unneeded component styles.

- **Simple and lively design**: Styled components enable props and global themes, making styling much easier than manually grouping many classes.

- **Reproducible styles**: When you style with the styled components, you can import your styles into the other project areas; it does not matter how big or small your codebase is.

CREATING AND STYLING: A COMMON WEB PAGE USING STYLED COMPONENTS

This section will produce a clone for the *disney+* landing page and add CSS to its components using the styled components.

First, we need to create an application in React that will contain our landing page.

Within the folder of your choice, open the *command prompt* and type the following command:

```
npx create-react-app Disney-landing-page
```

This will initialize and form our react app named Disney-landing-page by loading and installing all the React dependencies essential for our application.

Once all the dependencies have been installed, a development environment for the React app will be ready.

To get into the project folder, use the instruction below in the command prompt or the terminal of your code editor:

```
cd Disney-landing-page
```

INSTALLING STYLED COMPONENTS

Next, we need to install the styled components and the react-router-dom libraries into our project by means of the commands below:

```
yarn add styled-components
yarn add react-router-dom
```

STARTING THE DEVELOPMENT SERVER

Run one of the two commands on your console to start the application's development server, depending on which package manager you're using.

```
yarn start
npm start
```

With everything set up for our project, we can now open our project in a code editor and begin typing some code.

CREATING OUR COMPONENT

First, we need to form a folder to save our components. Within the *src* folder in your project edifice, create a folder and name its *components.*

In your newly created components folder, form two files and name: one *Landing.js* and the other *Header.js*. Next, we will make our components and style them within these two documents, as we will see briefly.

Before moving further, we start working with the CSS-in-JS (Styled-components), open the *Landing.js* file, and add the subsequent code to form our first component.

We form the Landing.js component with the code below:

import styled from "styled-components"; the styled component library
we installed is neccessary here!

This component will render landing page contents in the container.

```
const Landing = (props)=>{ // a functional component
  return
    (<Container>
    <Content>
    <Content>
    </Container>);
}
export default Landing;
```

To make our second component, open the Header.js file in the component folder.

Add the following code to the file:

```
import styled from "styled-components";
// This component will render the Navbar before
                          styling.
const Header = (props)=>{
  return (
  <Nav>
    Header
  </Nav>
  );
}
export default Header;
```

ROUTING A COMPONENT INTO THE MAIN APP

To get things started, let us open App.js, which is the base of our app. Then, we substitute all the content in it with the code below to produce an app function that will load our styled components and render them as the landing page.

After designing components/pages in your web apps, you may need to expose and allow your users to navigate through them. To achieve this, you require a dedicated router.

- *React Router* is the standard library for dynamic routing of components/page views in simple ReactJs apps like single-page web apps.

- *React Router* keeps the UIs and URLs synchronized, giving users seamless navigation in web apps.

To route components into the main application, you will import attributes from the react-router-dom, a React-router package that we installed earlier.

Import {BrowserRouter as Router, Switch, Route} from "react-router-dom"; The Router, Switch, and Route will help us move between our formed component and the main App.js.

Import Landing from "./components/Landing" This is to import the component formed in the Landing.js file.

Import Header from "./components/Header" This is to import the component formed in the Header.js file.

Import './App.css'; Load a set of predefined CSS that will define how HTML elements in the landing page behave.

```
function App() {    //main app
 return(
 <div>
 <Router>
  <Switch>
   <Route exact path="/">
   </Route>
  </Switch>
 </Router>
 </div>)
export default App;
```

This component will render a Navbar before the styling.

Now that we have formed our components, it is time to route it into the App.js.

To do so, add the codes between the *Route tags* as shown below:

```
<Landing/>
<Header/>
```

The final App.js should now consist of the following code:

```
import {BrowserRouter as Router, Switch, Route} from
        "react-router-dom";
import Landing from "./components/Landing";
import Header from "./components/Header";
import './App.css'

function App() {
 return(
 <div>
  <Router>
   <Switch>
    <Route path="/">
      <Landing/>
      <Header/>
    </Route>
   </Switch>
```

```
 </Router>
 </div>)
}
export default App;
```

ONTO SOME STYLING NOW

Be sure to form an images folder inside the public folder of the app.

You should have the landing page background images (BgImage), Disney+ icon image, logoOne, and logoTwo within the folder.

Let us add some cool attributes to our designed components (Landing and Header) and style them using the styled components depending on what content they hold.

Add the subsequent code between the Content tags in the Landing.js component.

```
<BgImage/>{/*holder for the landing page back-
          ground image should be here*/}
  <CTA>
    <LogoOne src="images/cta-logo-one.svg" alt='' />
           {/*holder for your logo-one should be
           here, to be styled as imgage*/}
    <Signup>GET IT ALL HERE</Signup>
    <Description> {/*holder for the paragraph of
                 text to be styled as p tag*/}
     Get premium access to Raya and the live IPL
                 matches with a Disney+ subscription.
                 As of 03/05/2020
      , the cost of Disney+ and the Disney bundle
                 will increment by $2.
    </Description>
    <LogoTwo src = "images/cta-logo-two.png" alt=''
            /> {/*holder for your logo-two should be
            here, to be styled as image*/}
  </CTA>
```

Next, add the codes below between the Nav tags in the Header.js component.

```
  <Logo>
    <img src="/images/logo.svg" alt= "Disney+"/>
  </Logo>
```

For styling the Container, Content area, Paragraph, Button, and Images in our Landing.js components, write the following CSS-in-JS directly after the line, *export the default Landing.*

STYLING THE CONTAINER

CSS attributes like overflow, flex, text-alignment, and others may be used to build up the layout for items in the container, as demonstrated in the next section.

```
{/*Container is declared in JS and styled and a
section is assigned to it*/}
{/*then CSS codes are written within backticks to act
on the Container*/}

const Container = styled.section`
overflow: hidden;
display: flex;
flex-direction: column;
text-align: center;
height: 100vh;
`;
```

Styling the Content Area

Set the height and position of the components in the content area to create space around them, and utilize CSS attributes like margin, height, width, padding, and position for extra customization.

```
{/*Content is declared in JS and styled.div is
          associate to it*/}
{/*CSS code is written within backticks(tagged-
          template literals) to render all content
          inside in a div*/}
const Content = styled.div`
margin-bottom: 10vw;
width: 100%;
position: relative;
min-height: 100vh;
box-sizing: border-box;
display: flex;
justify-content: center;
align-items: center;
```

```
flex-direction: column;
padding: 80px 40px;
height: 100%;
`;
```

STYLING THE BACKGROUND IMAGE

CSS properties like background size and z-index will allow you to set the image to cover the full div and give other elements priority over the image, respectively; we can also design background-position from the image.

```
{/*BgImage is defined in JS and styled.div is
associated to it*/}
{/*CSS code is written within the backticks(tagged-
            template literals) to render the image
            inside a div*/}

const BgImage = styled.div`
height: 100%;
background-position: top;
background-size: cover;
background-repeat: no-repeat;
position: absolute;
background-image: url("images/back-ground.jpg");
{/*the image is loaded as a URL*/}
top: 0;
left: 0;
right: 0;
z-index: -1
`;
```

STYLING THE CALL TO ACTION (CTA) AREA

To align in the center all elements in the CTA area, we will set margin-right and margin-left as auto, and justify-content enforces the center alignment of the elements in CTA.

CSS properties like max-width and margin will permit us to set the attention area for elements.

```
{/*The CTA will hold both these two logos and the
explanation. It is styled as a div*/}
const CTA = styled.div`
margin-bottom: 2vw;
```

```
max-width: 650px;
display:flex;
flex-direction:column;
flex-wrap: wrap;
justify-content: center;
margin-top: 0;
margin-right: auto;
margin-left: auto;
text-align: center;
`;
```

STYLING LOGOONE

The image in LogoOne requires to have no background color, have a height and width of specific pixels, and also have margin space between it and the elements below.

To achieve the above styling, use the CSS properties as below:

```
{/*LogOne styled as the image to render the img tag*/}
{/*CSS is to define height, width, margin*/}
const LogoOne = styled.img`
margin-bottom : 12px;
background-color: none;
max-width: 700px;
min-height: 60px;
display: block;
width: 100%;
`;
```

Styling the Sign Up Button

We will use the *hover selector* to form a button with the hover effect and display a background color on the hover.

```
{/*SignUp is styled to wrap around the text and appear
as button. It is designed as an anchor tag*/}
{/*CSS is to used to define how it should look*/}
const Signup = styled.a`
font-weight: bold;
color: #f9f9f9;
background-color: #0063e5;
margin-bottom: 12px;
width: 100%;
letter-spacing: 1.5px;
```

```
font-size: 25px;
padding: 16.5px 0;
border: 1px solid transparent;
border-radius: 4px;

&:hover{
  background-color :#0483ee;
}
`;
```

STYLING THE DESCRIPTION

To set font size, line height, letter spacing, margin, and color for the text in the description, we will use the CSS properties.

```
{/*holder for the paragraph of text to be styled as in
p tag. This will render the styled paragraph*/}
const Description = styled.p`
color: hsla(0, 0%, 95.3%, 1);
font-size: 14px;
margin: 0 0 24px;
line-height: 1.5em;
letter-spacing: 1.5;
`;
```

STYLING LOGOTWO

The image in LogoTwo should match in the styling needs similar to that done in styling LogoOne.

```
{/*It is styled as the image to render img tag*/}
{/*CSS is define height, width, margin*/}
const LogoTwo = styled.img`
margin-bottom : 23px;
max-width: 750px;
min-height: 67px;
display: inline-block;
vertical-align: top;
width: 90%;
`;
```

Edit the Header.js file immediately after the *export default Header* code to style the Nav and Logo in our Header component.

STYLING THE NAV FUNCTION

```
{/*To style .nav to render the Nav tag*/}
const Nav = styled.nav`
position: fixed;  //sets the nav fun as fixed
irrespective of any scroll behaviour.
top: 0;
left: 0;
right: 0;
height:70px;        //define height of the navbar fun
background-color: #090b13; //gives the
navbar background a color
display: flex;
justify-content: space-between; //creates the space
between nav the elements
align-items: center;
padding: 0 36px;
letter-spacing: 18px;
z-index:3;  //sets priority level for navbar against
other elements
`;

{/*Styling the Logo with .a to render image as an
anchor*/}
const Logo = styled.a`
padding:0;
width:80px;
margin-top:4px;
max-height:70px;
display: inline-block;
font-size:0;

img{
  display: block;
  width:100%;

};
```

SUMMARY

In this tutorial, we covered the library-styled component and its merits. The simple design and easy combination of styling within the React codebase make the development process more efficient. We ended up forming a simple landing page styled using styled components.

Return the Falsy Expression

In the below example, <div>0</div> will be returned by the render method.

```
render() {
 const count = 0;
 return (
  <div>
   {count && <h1>Messages: {count}</h1>}
  </div>
 );
}
```

Inline If-Else with Conditional Operator

Another process for conditionally rendering elements inline is to use the JS conditional operator condition? true: false.

In the below example, we use it to temporarily render a small block of text.

```
render() {
 const isLoggedIn = this.state.isLoggedIn;
 return (
  <div>
   The user is {isLoggedIn ? 'currently' : 'not'}
            logged in.
  </div>
 );
}
```

It can also be used for the larger expressions although it is less obvious what's going on.

```
render() {
 const isLoggedIn = this.state.isLoggedIn;
 return (
  <div>
   {isLoggedIn
    ? <LogoutButton onClick={this.handleLogoutClick} />
    : <LoginButton onClick={this.handleLoginClick} />
   }
```

```
    </div>
  );
}
```

Just like in JS, it is up to you to pick a suitable style based on what you and your team consider more readable. Also remember that whenever conditions become too composite, it might be a good time to abstract a component.

PREVENTING COMPONENT FROM RENDERING

In rare cases, you might need a component to hide even though it was rendered by the other component, and to do this, return null instead of its render output.

In the below example, the <WarningBanner /> is rendered dependent on the value of the prop termed as warn, and if the value of the prop is false, then the component does not render.

```
function WarningBanner(props) {
  if (!props.warn) {
    return null;
  }

  return (
    <div className="warning">
     Warning!
    </div>
  );
}

class Page extends React.Component {
  constructor(props) {
    super(props);
    this.state = {showWarning: true};
    this.handleToggleClick = this.handleToggleClick.b
                             ind(this);
  }

  handleToggleClick() {
    this.setState(state => ({
     showWarning: !state.showWarning
    }));
  }
```

```
render() {
  return (
   <div>
    <WarningBanner warn={this.state.showWarning} />
    <button onClick={this.handleToggleClick}>
    {this.state.showWarning ? 'Hide' : 'Show'}
    </button>
   </div>
  );
 }
}

ReactDOM.render(
 <Page />,
 document.getElementById('root')
);
```

STYLING COMPONENTS IN REACT

React is a fantastic JavaScript library for creating rich user interfaces. It offers a great component abstraction for establishing your interfaces into well-functioning codes, but what about the look and feel of the application? There are numerous ways of styling React components from using stylesheets to using external styling libraries.

Styling React components over the years has enhanced and become much easier with various methods and strategies. This section will demonstrate how to style React components using four fundamental styling methodologies, along with examples of how to utilize them. I'll discuss the advantages and drawbacks of different styling options in the procedure, and by the conclusion of this part, you'll know everything there is to know about styling React components and how they function, as well as the numerous ways that can be used to style these components.

Note: A fundamental understanding of ReactJS and CSS would be good to have for this section.

WHAT DOES "STYLING" IN REACT APPS EVEN MEAN?

The reason you will style your React app is the same as the reason you will style other web pages and web applications you have been working on. Styling in React apps describes how React components or elements appear on screen or in other media.

The whole essence of building front-end user interfaces with React is how flexible it is to create these UIs, especially as components, and also style them to give us a great look and experience and it is important to know that whatever styling approaches you may decide to use in still CSS - you are writing the CSS as you have always done. The difference is that the strategies (which we will be looking at) help make the procedure easy because of the exclusivity of React.

Major Styling Strategies in React #

There are numerous strategies to follow when planning to style React components, these strategies have also enhanced and evolved over the years. In this part, we'll go over the most common and up-to-date stylistic strategies, as well as how to apply them to React components. Among these styling methods are:

1. **CSS and SCSS stylesheets**: They entail employing distinct stylesheets, similar to how we conservatively style our HTML web pages or applications with CSS or a CSS compiler called SASS.

2. **CSS modules**: A CSS component is a CSS file that comprises class and animation names, which are by default scoped locally.

3. **Styled components**: Styled components are the library for React and React Native that permit you to use component-level styles in your app that are written with a mixture of JavaScript and CSS using a method called CSS-in-JS.

4. **JSS**: JSS is a CSS writing tool that lets you utilize JavaScript to specify styles in a declarative, conflict-free, and recyclable manner. It can build in the browser, on the server, or in Node at build time.

CHAPTER 4

Handling Images

IN THIS CHAPTER

- ➤ Images
- ➤ Importing images
- ➤ Inside public Folder
- ➤ Using Public Folder
- ➤ Inside src Folder

IMPORTING IMAGES

In this chapter, we will study how to use an image or picture with JSX component and HTML file using "img" tag in ReactJS file. Adding an image with the JSX component in ReactJs is crucial for any developer or designer. In the React App default directory structure, you will get two options to upload your images file:

- Inside *public* folder
- Inside *src* folder

INSIDE PUBLIC FOLDER

If you insert a file in the public folder, it will not be processed by Webpack. Instead, it will copy in the build folder without any external Changement.

DOI: 10.1201/9781003309369-4

To reference or access assets in the public folder, you will need a particular variable called "PUBLIC_URL." You can only access the picture using the %PUBLIC_URL% prefix from the "public folder."

Generally, I recommend importing fonts, stylesheets, and images from JavaScript.

```
<link rel="favicon_icons" href="%PUBLIC_URL%/favicons
                             .ico"/>
<link rel="stylesheet" type="text/css" href="%PUBLIC_
                             URL%/style.css"/>
```

Notes

- None of the files or scripts in the public folder get minimized or post-processed.

- Missing files will not be called or triggered during compilation, resulting in 404 errors for your users.

- Because result filenames will not include content hashes, you will need to add or rename query parameters whenever they change.

USING THE PUBLIC FOLDER

- In the build output, you will require a file with a specific name, such as manifest.webmanifest.

- You will have hundreds of photos and need to dynamically reference their paths.

- You'd want to add a short script, such as custom.js, outside of the packaged code.

- Some libraries may be incompatible with Webpack, in which case you must include it as a <script> tag.

For instance, if image is in Public Folder,

index.html

```
<img src="%PUBLIC_URL%/mypic.jpg" alt="mypic"/>
```

```
//if image is in the another folder under public
          folder like :public/images then
```

```
<img src="%PUBLIC_URL%/images/mypic1.jpg" alt="mypic"/>
```

App.js

For the JavaScript module, you should use {process.env.PUBLIC_URL} in place of %PUBLIC_URL%.

```
<img src={process.env.PUBLIC_URL + "/mypics.jpg"}
     alt="mypic"/>
<img src={process.env.PUBLIC_URL + "/images/mypics.j
     pg"} alt="mypics"/>
```

INSIDE THE FOLDER "SRC"

With Webpack, using static assets like fonts and images works very similar to CSS. You can import a file in a JavaScript module. This tells Webpack to include that particular file in the bundle. Unlike the CSS imports, importing a file will give you a string value. Now this value is the final path you can reference in your code. For example, the src attribute of an image or the *href* of a link to a PDF.

Notes

- Script and stylesheet get decreased and bundled, composed to evade additional network requirements.

- Mislaid files cause compiling faults instead of 404 errors for your users.

- Consequently, computer filename contains satisfied hashes, so you don't need to worry about browsers caching their old versions.

HOW TO USE

This confirms that Webpack will appropriately transfer the images into the build folder and deliver us with the right routes when the project is erected.

App.js

```
import pic from './mypic.jpg';
<img src={pic} alt="mypic"/>
```

Example Code

```
import React, {Component} from "react";
import ReactDOM from "react-dom";
import logo from "./abc.png";
class Employee extends Component{
render(){
 return(
  <>
  <h2>Inside Public Folder</h2>
 <img src={process.env.PUBLIC_URL+"tutorials-website
         -logo.png"} alt="image inserting concept"/>
 <h2>Inside src Folder</h2>
 <img src={logo} alt="tutorialswebsite logo"/>
  </>
 );
 }
}
 ReactDOM.render(<Employee/>, document.
         getElementById("root"));
```

CONCLUSION

If you need to design an e-commerce website where you want to upload many pictures, I will suggest you use the "Public Folder." You can't use the *src* folder due to some safety measures.

CHAPTER 5

React Routers

IN THIS CHAPTER

➢ Routing

➢ Router and query parameters

React Router is the standard library for routing in React. It empowers the navigation among views of various components in the React app; it also permits changing the browser URL and keeps the user interface in sync with the URL. It is a standard library system built on top of React and is also used to generate routing in the React app using React Router Package (RRP). It gives the synchronous URL on the browser with data or info that will display on the web page. It maintains the standard structure and behavior of the app and is mainly used for developing single-page web apps.

Routing is how a user is directed to different pages based on their action or requests. ReactJS Router is primarily used for developing single-page web apps. React Router is used to define the multiple routes in the app. When a user enters the exact URL into the browser and if that URL path matches any "route" within the router file, the user will be redirected to that route.

Routing is the ability to move between several parts of an app when the user enters a URL or clicks on an element (link, button, icon, image, etc.) within the app.

Until this point, you have dealt with the simple projects that do not need transitioning from one view to the other; thus, you are yet to cooperate with Routing in React.

DOI: 10.1201/9781003309369-5

This chapter introduces routing in a React app. To extend your apps by adding the routing capabilities, you will use the popular react-router library. It is worth noting that this library has three variants:

1. **react-router**: It is the core library.

2. **react-router-dom**: It is a variant of the core library meant to be used for web apps.

3. **react-router-native**: It is a variant of the core library used with the react-native in the development of Android and iOS apps.

NEED FOR REACT ROUTER

React Router plays an essential role in displaying multiple views in a single-page app. Without the React Router, it is impossible to display multiple views in React apps. Most social media websites like Facebook and Instagram use the React Router to render multiple views.

REACT ROUTER INSTALLATION

React contains three different packages for routing:

1. **react-router**: It provides the core routing components or methods and functions for the React Router apps.

2. **react-router-native**: It is used for mobile apps.

3. **react-router-dom**: It is used for web apps design.

It is not feasible to include React Router in your app directly. To utilize React routing, you must first install the react-router-dom modules in your project. The react-router-dom is installed with the command below:

$ npm install react-router-dom --save

COMPONENTS IN REACT ROUTER

Router components are classified into two types:

1. **<BrowserRouter>**: It is used to handle dynamic URLs.

2. **<HashRouter>**: It is used for handling static requests.

Depending on the scenario, it is not always required to install the core react-router library by itself, but rather to choose between react-router-dom and react-router-native. All of the functionality of the core react-router libraries is imported by both react-router-dom and react-router-native.

The choice of this book is in the realm of web apps, so we can carefully select react-router-dom. This library is installed in the project by running the command below in the project directory or file:

```
npm install --save react-router-dom
```

Routers

The react-router package includes the number of routers that we can benefit from depending on the platform we aim for. These include BrowserRouter, HashRouter, and MemoryRouter.

For the browser-based apps we are building or designing, the BrowserRouter and HashRouter are a good fit.

The BrowserRouter is used for apps with a dynamic server that understands how to handle various sorts of URLs, whereas the HashRouter is used for static websites with a server that only replies to requests for files it knows about.

Moving further, we shall use the BrowserRouter with the postulation that the server running our app is dynamic and worth noting in that any router expects to receive only a child. Take the below example:

```
ReactDOM.render(
  <BrowserRouter>
   <App/>
  </BrowserRouter>,
  document.getElementById('root'));
```

In this example, the <App/> module is the child to the <BrowserRouter> and should be the only child. Now, the routing can happen from anywhere within the <App/> module, though it is considered good practice to group and place all the paths in the same place.

History

Each router creates the history object to keep track of the current location and re-renders the app whenever this location varies. For this reason, the other React Routers component relies on this history object being extant; this is why they are required to be rendered inside a router.

The HTML5 history API (Application Programming Interface) is used by the BrowserRouter to keep the user interface UI in sync with the URL inside the browser address bar.

The history object formed by the Router contains the number of properties and one of the position properties whose value is also the object. We should emphasize the location attribute in this chapter because the others are outside the scope of this book.

When the preceding example is shown in the browser, the produced history object should be visible in the React DevTools window, as seen below.

- The location of object within history object is molded so

  ```
  { pathname, search, hash, state }
  ```

- The location object properties or characteristics are derived from the app URL.

Routes

The <Route/> module is one of the most significant building blocks in the React Router package or suite. It renders the proper user interface UI when the present location matches the route's path. The path is the prop on the <Route/> module that defines the pathname that the route should match as shown in the following example:

```
<Route path="/items"/>
```

This route is matched when pathname is /items or all the other paths that start with /items/ for example /items/2. If the intention is to match only /items firmly, the <Route/> component receives the exact prop. Adding this confirms that only the pathname that precisely matches the current location is rendered. Let us consider the example below that uses the exact prop.

```
<Route exact path="/items" />
```

When the path is matched, a React component or module should be rendered so that there is a change in the UI.

It is also worth observing that the react-router package uses the Path-to-RegExp package to turn the path string into the regular expression and matched against the current location.

The <Route/> component or module offers three props that can be used to determine which component to render:

- => component
- => render
- => children

Component Prop

The component prop expresses that the Route will return the React element when the path is coordinated. This React element is formed from the provided component or module using React.createElement. There is an example using the component prop.

```
<Route
 exact
 path="/items"
 component={Items}
/>
```

In this example, the Items components will be returned when the path matches the present location.

Render Prop

The render prop provides the capability for inline rendering and passing extra props to the element and this prop expects the function that returns a React element when the present location matches the route's route. There are examples demonstrating the use of the render prop on the Route component.

```
<Route
 exact
 path="/items"
 render={() => (<div>List of Items</div>)}
/>
```

In the above example, when the existing location matches the route exactly, a React element is formed and the string List of Items is rendered into the browser.

```
const cat = {category: "food"}
<Route
 exact path="/items"
 render={props => <Items {...props} data={cat}/>}
/>
```

In the second example, data or info represents the extra props that are passed to the Items component. Here, the cat is passed as an extra prop.

Children Prop

The children prop is like the render prop, which at all times expects a function that returns the React element. The leading difference is that the element defined by the child prop is returned for all routes regardless of whether the present location matches the route or not.

```
<Route children={props => <Items {...props}/>}/>
```

In the above case, Items components are always rendered.

Switch

The react-router library also encompasses a <Switch/> component that is used to wrap multiple <Route/> components into it. The Switch component selects the first matched path from all of its children's pathways.

The next example validates how multiple routes or paths act in the absence of the Switch components.

```
<Route
path="/items"
render={() => (<div><em>List of the items</em></
div>)}
/>
<Route
path="/items/3"
render={() => (<div>Item with id of 3</div>)}
/>
```

In the browser, when you navigate for /items/3, the React elements in both Route components will be rendered as shown below:

- List of items

- An item with id of 3

This could be the envisioned behavior, where the first component displays the label and the other paths with the same base route render different user interfaces.

Let us modify the above example and include the <Switch/> component and observe the behavior when we navigate to /items/4.5.

```
<Switch>
 <Route
  path="/items"
  render={() => (<div><em>List of the items</em></
div>)}
 />
 <Route
  path="/items/4.5"
  render={() => (<div>Item with id of 4.5</div>)}
 />
</Switch>
```

In the browser, only the List of Items will render and this is because the Switch component matches only the first route that matches the current position. In this example, the route /items have matched when /items/4.5 entered the browser's address bar.

Link

The react-router package also contains the <Link/> component used to direct the different fragments of an app through hyperlinks. It is like the HTML's anchor element, but the key difference is that using the Link component does not reload the page but changes the user interface. Using an anchor tag would need the page to reload to load the new user interface. When the Link component is clicked, it also updates the URL.

Let us explore the use of the Link components further by creating the app that permits us to navigate between the categories and items.

```
export const Home = () => (
 <div>
  Home Component
  <ul>
   <li>
    <Link to="/items">Items</Link>
   </li>
   <li>
    <Link to="/category">Category</Link>
   </li>
  </ul>
 </div>
);
```

The Home component contains the links to the Items and Categories component.

The <Link/> components may be used as a prop to describe the position to direct to. This prop can either be the string or a location object. If it is a string, it is transformed to a location object, and note that the pathname must be absolute.

To get an example set up on your machine, copy the project here and run npm install && npm start.

Clicking on the Items link triggers a user interface variation and updates the URL in the address bar.

Likewise, clicking on the Class link triggers a user interface that modifies and updates the URL into the address bar.

NESTED ROUTING

Now that you understand the <Route/> component and route function, we can move on to layered routing in a React project.

A match object is formed when the router's route and position are effectively matched. This object contains info about the URL and the route. This info can be retrieved as properties on the matching entity.

Let's look at the properties:

- => **URL** : The string that returns the matched portion of the URL

- => **path** : The string that returns the route's route

- => **isExact** : The boolean that returns true (1) if the match was exact

- => **params** : The object comprising key-value couples that were coordinated by the Path-To-RegExp package.

Using a Route tester to match paths to URLs, you can try this out.

To do nested routing properly, we employ match.URL for nested Links as well as match.path for nested Routes.

Let us explore the use of nested routing by working on the example. Copy the project here and run npm install && npm start to get it set up and fired up.

This example comprises four components:

1. Header components which contain the Home, Items, and Category links

2. Home component which contains dummy data

3. Items component which contains a list of dummy items

4. Category component which demonstrates nested routing and dynamic routing

We shall focus on the Category components since it contains the nested and dynamic routing.

```
export const Category = ({match}) => (
 <div>
 <h1>Category Component</h1>
 <h5>Click on a category</h5>
 <ul>
  <li>
   <Link to={`${match.url}/shoes`}>Shoe</Link>
  </li>
  <li>
   <Link to={`${match.url}/food`}>Foods</Link>
  </li>
  <li>
   <Link to={`${match.url}/dresses`}>Dress</Link>
  </li>
 </ul>
);
```

Based on the codes snippet above, when the Category link is clicked, a route path is matched and a match object is formed and sent as the prop to the Category components.

Within the Category components, the match object is destructured in the argument list, and links to the three categories are formed using match.URL.

Template literals are used to construct or design the value of the prop on the Link components to the different /shoe, /foods, and /dress URLs.

Opening the above example in a browser and clicking on the category link indicate three separate categories; when any of these categories is clicked, the URL changes, but the user interface remains unchanged.

To address this fault or errors and guarantee that the user interface changes when a category link is visited, we create a dynamic route within the Category components that utilizes match.path as its path parameter and then dynamically update the user interface.

```
<Route
 path={`${match.path}/:categoryName`}
 render={props =>
        (<div>
          {props.match.params.categoryName} category
        </div>
        )
    }
/>
```

When you examine the value of the path prop in the above code snippet, you will notice that we use:categoryName, a variable within the routename. The path parameter inside the supplied URL is categoryName, and it collects anything that occurs after '/'category.

:categoryName is the path parameter within the given URL and it catches everything that comes after '/'category.

Passing the values to the path prop in this way saves us from having to hardcode all the different category routes and notice the use of template literals to construct the right path.

A pathname like category/shoes forms a parameter object like the one below:

```
{
categoryName: "shoe"
}
```

The render prop in the route example runs the inline render which displays the categoryName param from the matched object contained within props.

That should fix the issue of unchanging user interface, and now clicking on one of the groups should trigger an update of both the URL and the user interface.

Protected Routes

The rationale for having the protected route or paths is that when any user tries to access part of the app without logging in, they are redirected to the login page to sign in to the app.

For this re-direct to work as intended, the react-router package provides the <Redirect/> component to serve this purpose, and this component has to prop which is passed to it in the form of an object comprising the path-name and state as shown below:

```
<Redirect
  to={{pathname: '/login', state: {from:props.location}}}
/>
```

Here, the Redirect component or module replaces the present location in the stack with the path name provided in the object (/login) and then saves the location that the user was attempting to visit, in the state's property. The values in the state can be retrieved from within the Login components using this.props.location.state.

For example, if the user attempts to navigate to /admin, a protected route, without log in first, they will be redirected to the login page. Following the successful sign-in, they will be redirected to /admin, the route they intended to visit in the first place.

Custom Routes

In order to attain the concept of protected routes, we must first understand how to form custom routes.

Custom routes are an extravagant way of saying nesting a route inside the component, and this is typically done when there is a need to choose whether the components should render or not.

In the case of the protected route, a given route should only be retrieved when a user is logged in; else, the user should be directed to the login page.

Let us explore custom routes more in the other example: copy the project here and run npm install && npm start to set up.

The private route is also assembled with all other routes as shown below.

The private route has the path, and components and is authenticated props. Let us take a look at the private (custom) route.

We destructure the props within the argument list and rename components to Component, and we use the Route component by passing it to the ...rest and render props. We write code in the render prop that determines whether to render the component and which one to render if the user is logged in. Otherwise, the user is sent back to the login page.

Within its render method, the Login component contains a fake authentication method or technique that logs the user in when they click Login button. See the code excerpt from the Login component below.

The redirectToReferrer state property is set to the true value when the user is signed in. This triggers the redirect to the route they had proposed to visit, or to the '/' path in case they crossed straight to the login route and

Run npm start if you don't already have a project running and navigate to localhost:3000. You should see this.

Clicking on Admin link when not signed in redirects you to the /login page, displaying the login button.

After clicking the login button, you are redirected to the protected admin page.

ROUTER AND QUERY PARAMETERS

Query parameters are a definite set of parameters committed to the end of the URL. They are key=value pairs we can assign to a URL, used as one of several ways to pass data to an app. React Router recommends using a library like query-string, which is available on npm if you cannot use the built-in browser procedure of the URL API and must run yarn add query-string to add and install it. Parsing query strings is then quite simple as passing location.search into the parse() function.

How to Get Query String Values in the
JavaScript JS with URLSearchParams

1. const params = new URLSearchParams(window. location. search)

2. params. has('test')

3. params. get('test')

4. const params = new URLSearchParams(window. location. search)
for (const param of params) { console. log(param) }

Getting Parameters from URL in the React Application

1. Sample address like: http://localhost:3000/?id=55&name=test. const queryParams = new URLSearchParams(window. ...

2. import React, { Component } from 'react'; import { BrowserRouter as Router, Switch, Route } from the 'react-router-dom'; ...

3. Functional components. ...

4. Class components.

How Do You Pass the Parameter in a Query?

Any word after the question mark (?) in the URL is considered to be the parameter that can grasp values. The value for the consistent parameter is given after the symbol "equals" (=). Multiple parameters can pass through the URL by separating them with several "&" symbols.

Dealing with the Router and Query Params

There are two different concepts or methods that interest us: the first is router parameters, and the second one is query parameters. What are these concepts? A router parameter is the part of your URL and can look like the following:

```
/products/111
/users/1/products
#Router params
```

In the first case, we query against the resource /products and is being looking for the particular item 111.

In the second case, we're looking for resource users and specific users whose id is 1.

Router parameters are part of your URL. Typically, we have a user directly to a page and if needed, we dig out the router parameter, cause requests to be part of our query, and imagine that the link /products/111 is clicked on. This will mean that we will take the user to the ProductDetail components where we will need to:

```
dig out the router parameters
pose the query based on said param and show the result
class ProductDetail extends React.Component {
```

```
state = {
 product: void 0
}
async componentDidMount() {
 const product1 = await api.getProduct(`/products
/${this.props.match.params.id}`);
 this.setState({
  product1,
 });
}
render() {
 return (
  <React.Fragment>
   {this.state.product &&
   <div>{this.state.product1.name}</div>
   }
  </React.Fragment>
 );
}
}
```

The exciting part here is how we admitted the router parameter:

```
this.props.match.params.id
```

The match object comprises a params object that points to our router parameter id.

Let us quickly remind ourselves how this router was set up:

```
<Route path='/products/:id'
component={ProductDetail}/>
```

Above, you can see that we define route /products/:id, and thereby we set the wild-card to :id, which makes it possible to access it in codes by typing this.props.match.params.id.

#Query params

Let us talk about query parameters next. A query parameter is used to filter down the resource and the typical example is using parameters like pageSize or page to specify to the backend that only want a small slice of the content and not the full list on which can be millions of rows potentially and query parameters are found after ? characters in the URL which would make the URL look as /products?page=1&pageSize=20. Let us have a look in codes at how we access query parameters:

```
import React from 'react';
import { parse } from 'query-string';
class Products extends React.Component {
 state = {
  products: []
 };

async componentDidMount() {
   const { location: { search } } = this.props;
   const { page, pageSize } = search;
   const products = await api.getProducts(`/product
                 s?page=${page}&pageSize=${pageSize}`);
   this.setState({
    products,
   });
 }
 render() {
  <React.Fragment>
  {this.props.products.map(product => <div>{product
                                .name}</div>)}
  </React.Fragment>
 }
}
```

As you have seen above, we can access the query parameters through a location object that sits on the search object that represents our parameters like the following:

```
{
 page: 1,
 pageSize: 22
}
Programmatic routing >
```

Let us consider the example of Routing and query parameters:

```
import React from "react";
import {
```

```
BrowserRouter as Router,
Link,
useLocation
} from "react-router-dom";

// React Router does not have any sentiments about
// how you should analyze URL query strings.
//
// If you use the simple key=value query strings and
// you don't need to support IE 11, you can use
// the browser's built-in URLSearchParams API.
//
// If query strings contain the array or object
// syntax, you will probably need to bring your own
// query parsing functions.

export default function QueryParamsExample() {
 return (
  <Router>
   <QueryParamsDemo />
  </Router>
 );
}

// A custom hook that builds up on useLocation to
parse
// the query strings for you.
function useQuery() {
 const { search } = useLocation();

 return React.useMemo(() => new
            URLSearchParams(search), [search]);
}

function QueryParamsDemo() {
 let query = useQuery();

 return (
  <div>
   <div>
    <h2>Accounts section</h2>
    <ul>
```

```
      <li>
       <Link to="/account?name=netflix">Netflix
                              Account</Link>
      </li>
      <li>
       <Link to="/account?name=zillow-group">Zillow
                              Group</Link>
      </li>
      <li>
        <Link to="/account?name=yahoo">Yahoo</Link>
      </li>
      <li>
        <Link to="/account?name=modus-create">Modus
                              Create</Link>
      </li>
     </ul>

     <Child name={query.get("name")} />
    </div>
   </div>
 );
}

function Child({ name }) {
 return (
  <div>
   {name ? (
    <h3>
     The <code>name</code> in the query string is
                              &quot;{name}
     &quot;
    </h3>
   ) : (
    <h3>There is no name in the query string</h3>
   )}
  </div>
 );
}
```

CHAPTER 6

Programmatic Navigation

IN THIS CHAPTER

➢ Programmatic navigation

➢ Lazy loading

Programmatic navigation means when a user is redirected as the result of an action that occurs on a route, like a login or sign-up action. In this chapter, we'll look at a variety of methodologies or strategies for exploring React Router programmatically.

The React ideology consists of three core methods – the user event, state management, and render function – and programmatic routing can be said to be in line with this ideology.

The effect of routing programmatically is on that particular page as no route altering or, at other times, may bring about the need to change a route. When there is a need, it is not going to be triggered by clicking a link, so we do not always have to use the Link component, and using the Link component in such a scenario is not optimal.

Sometimes we want a specific action: we only want to travel to a different route when a certain event occurs or when a user completes an activity, such as submitting a form that takes you to a new page, and we call this type of action programmatic navigation.

DOI: 10.1201/9781003309369-6

React Router is designed or created to follow the ideology mentioned previously. Thus, programmatically navigating with the React Router should, by definition, align with those three core concepts or methods.

React Router provides us with the history object, which is accessible by passing this object into each route as a prop. This history object allows us to manually control the history of the browser. Since React Router alters what we see based on the current URL, the history object gives us fine-grained control over when or where separate pieces of the app are shown.

WHAT IS PROGRAMMATIC NAVIGATION?

Programmatic navigation refers to when the user is redirected as a result of an action that occurs on a route. Login or sign-up action or form submission action on a route is a typical example of navigating programmatically. In this chapter, we'll look at a variety of ways and methods for exploring React Router programmatically. To programmatically navigate means to use JavaScript, i.e., program codes, a function, or a method call. If you just want the straight-up hyperlink, then your best bet is <Link to="/some-URL" />

HOW DO YOU ROUTE PROGRAMMATICALLY IN THE REACT?

With version v4 of React Router, there are three approaches or methods that you can take to programmatic routing within components:

1. Use the withRouter higher-order components.

2. Use configuration and render a <Route>.

3. Use the context.

Using Redirect Component

The primary way you programmatically navigate using the React Router v4+ is by using the <Redirect /> component, and it is a recommended process that helps the user navigate between routes.

Using the Redirect constituent is a different strategy or method, but it is just as acceptable, and the objective is to have it pointing at a state in the module and then traverse if that condition is met.

Some may argue that this solution requires more effort because it requires creating a new prop based on the component's state and adding a condition to the render process to determine when to render the Redirect constituent. This is true, yet there is a reasonable counterargument from those who prefer explicit to implicit. It implies that explicitly declaring and altering your state is preferable to the implicit state handled by the imperative API such as history.push, which we shall discuss later.

Here is a codes example of how to use the Redirect component/module:

Code-sandbox: https://codesandbox.io/s/gallant-meitner-bshng?file=/src/App.js

```
import React, { useState } from 'react';
import { Redirect } from 'react-router-dom';
import { userLogin } from './userAction';
import Form from './Form';
const Login = () => {
const [isLoggedIn, setIsLoggedIn] = useState(false);

const handleLogin = async (userDetail) => {
 const success = await userLogin(userDetail);
 if(success) setIsLoggedIn(true);
}

 if (isLoggedIn) {
  return <Redirect to='/profiles' />
 }
 return (
  <>
   <h1>Login here</h1>
   <Form onSubmit={handleLogin} />
  </>
 )
}
export default Login;
```

Using history.push() Method

history.push() is another approach or technique where we use the history props React Router provides while rendering the component.

In other words, this works when the components are being rendered by React Router, bypassing the component prop to the Route. If this is the scenario, the React Router sends the component three props: location, match, and history.

We'll concentrate on the history prop, which maintains track of all the session history beneath the hood and gives us several methods or approaches to change it.

The push method is crucial and is used to push a path as a route to the history stack, which performs as Last In First Out (LIFO). This causes the application to redirect to the last route added, redirecting the user to a detailed route. The below example assumes the component is rendered with the React Router.

Code-sandbox: https://codesandbox.io/s/angry-saha-djh3z?file=/src/App.js

```
import React from "react";
import { userLogin } from "./userAction";
import Form from "./Form";
const Login = props => {
const handleLogin = async userDetail => {
 const success = await userLogin(userDetail);
 if (success) props.history.push("/profile");
};
return (
 <>
  <h1>Login here</h1>
  <Form onSubmit={handleLogin} />
 </>
);
};
export default Login;
```

Using withRouter Method

We previously said that in order for a component to have access to props .history.push, it must have been rendered with the React Router. In other circumstances, this may not be the case. As a result, we render a component ourselves. To make the history property or attributes available to the components, the React Router team formed the Higher-Order Component (HOC) withRouter, and wrapping a component with this HOC expresses the properties.

Code-sandbox : https://codesandbox.io/s/silent-rain-l19lg?file=/src/App .js:0-442

```
import React from 'react';
import { withRouter } from 'react-router-dom';
import { userLogin } from './userAction';
import Form from './Form';

const Login = (props) => {
const handleLogin = async (userDetail) => {
 const success = await userLogin(userDetail);
 if(success) props.history.push('/profile');
}
return (
  <>
   <h1>Login here</h1>
   <Form onSubmit={handleLogin} />
  </>
 )
}
export default withRouter(Login);
```

Using the useHistory Hook

As of current versions of React Router (v5.1) and React (v16.8), we have a new method or process called the useHistory hook which embraces the power of the React Hooks, and this is used for programmatic navigation purposes within the functional component. The useHistory hook gives you access to the history instance, which we can use to move between pages regardless of whether the component was rendered by the React Router or not, and therefore eliminates the need for withRouter.

Code-sandbox : https://codesandbox.io/s/serene-cookies-hc629?file=/src/App.js

```
import { useHistory } from "react-router-dom";
const HomeButton = () =>{
let history = useHistory();
const handleClick = () => {
 history.push("/home");
}
return (
 <button type="button" onClick={handleClick}>
  Go home
 </button>
```

```
);
}
export default HomeButton;
```

CONCLUSION

The main focus of this portion was to share how you can safely navigate between apparatuses using the React Router package.

Given that React offers a declarative technique for designing user interfaces, utilizing Redirect is the suggested option for navigating when the Link cannot be utilized, but there is no harm in using any of the other approaches since they are all supported and semantically accurate.

Furthermore, with the introduction of useHistory as well as the other APIs in the 5.1.2 release, navigating programmatically becomes much easier as long as you understand how to use the React Hooks.

For example, here is how you could programmatically navigate the user after they have submitted a form:

```
import React, { useState } from 'react'

import { useNavigation } from 'react-navi'

export function NewForm() {

 let [name, setName] = useState('Spartacus')

 // `useNavigation()` returns a navigation object

 let navigation = useNavigation()

 let handleSubmit = (e) => {
  e.preventDefault()

  // You can also call `navigation.navigate()` to
                     navigate to the new page.

   navigation.navigate('/thankyou/'+encodeURICompon
                     ent(name))
 }
 return (
  <form onSubmit={handleSubmit}>
   <h1>Enter your full name</h1>
```

```
    <input value={name} onChange={e => setName
                           (e.target.value)} />
    <button>Ok</button>
  </form>
 )
}
export function Thankyou so much({ name }) {
 return (
  <h1>Thankyou, {name}!</h1>
 )
}
/
```

BUILD-IN PROGRESS

Navi's navigation.navigate() method provides the promise to the new URL's Route object, making it ideal for usage in form submit handlers that require the promise as a response, such as react-final-form.

Another form handling example, this time utilizing react-final-form and POSTing the form, result in a map() handler so that the form may be processed server-side if JavaScript is disabled.

```
import { map, mount, redirect, route } from 'navi'
import React, { Suspense } from 'react'
import ReactDOM from 'react-dom'
import { Router } from 'react-navi'
import { Form, FormErrors, FormField, FormSubmitButton
} from './components'
async function login(name) {
 alert('trying login')
 if (name === 'Spartacus') {
  throw new Error("I do not believe you.")
 }
}
const loginRoute = map(async req => {
 let state = {}
 // If the request fails, save the error in the window
                       .history.state so
 // that re-running the route will not retry request.
 if (req.method === 'POST' && !req.state.error) {
  let name = req.body.name
  try {
   await login(name)
```

```
    return redirect('/thankyou so much/'+encodeURICompo
                nent(name))
  }
  catch (error) {
    state.error = error && error.message
  }
}

  return route({
    error: state.error,
    state,
    status: state.error ? 400 : 200,
    head: <title>Login here</title>,
    view: <Login here />
  })
})
function Login() {
  return (
    <Form method='POST' initialValues={{ name:
                                      'Spartacus' }}>
      <h1>Login here</h1>
/
```

LAZY LOADING

Lazy loading is not a new concept. It has been available for some time. In essence, lazy loading means that a constituent or a part of codes must get loaded when it is essential. It is also referred to as codes excruciating and data fetching. When we construct an application, the resultant bundle is frequently rather enormous as our project expands in size. This will impair the loading time of our program for those with low bandwidth connections, such as mobile users. For that reason, it's a good idea only to load as much of your app as you need.

What do we mean by that? Imagine your app consists of many routes and some routes you are likely to visit often and some not so much. If you direct your application to just load the routes required by the user at first load, you may bring in more routes when the user requests them. This is referred to as *lazy loading*, and we generate one bundle that serves as our initial app, followed by numerous little bundles as we visit the specific route. We'll need Web-pack and React to collaborate on this one.

Talking about React precisely, it bundles the complete codes and deploys all of them at the same time. Normally, this is not a terrible idea because React SPAs (single-page apps) are relatively modest and have no effect on the presentation, but what if we have a massive app, such as a content management system with a customer portal, admin portal, and so on. It doesn't seem like a good idea to load the entire program in this scenario.

It will be a huge app and will cost a lot of needless data transmission, making the website load slowly.

Because a user login will not have access to certain admin topographies, loading it is a waste of memory and work.

In this part, I will explain the advantages of lazy loading and how to implement it in React.

Why Is Lazy Loading (and Suspense) Important

First, bundling aligns our codes components in the development and puts them in one JavaScript JS portion that it passes to the browser. But as our app grows, we notice that the bundle gets very bulky in size. This can swiftly make using your app very hard and incredibly sluggish. With codes splitting, the bundle can split into smaller chunks where the most significant chunk can be loaded first and then every other inferior one lazily loaded.

Also, while building apps, we know that as a best practice, contemplation should be made for users using mobile internet data and others with really deliberate internet connections. We, the developers/designers, should always be able to regulate the user experience even during the suspense period when resources are being loaded to the DOM.

Advantages of Lazy Loading

When we know that certain codes/features will not be available to all the users or the user does not access them often, it is best to load them when the user needs them. This improves user experience and primary loading time.

For example, let us consider that our app has two sections, A and B. Size of A is 3 MB, and its loading time is about 3 seconds. As B is also 3 MB in size, its loading time is similarly 3 seconds, and we know that a user will visit either of the segments, or that a user receiving section A will seldom access section B, and vice versa. If we loaded the entire app at the start of our app, it would cost the user 6 MB of data and take 6 seconds to load. The user might not want to wait for 6 seconds or would not be happy that the site is costing them a lot of data, and this can be enhanced and halved with appropriate lazy loading.

Note: This is not the general case, and small single-page apps are typically in KBS.

Disadvantages of Lazy Loading

1. The extra lines of codes to be added to the present ones to implement lazy load makes the codes a bit complex.

2. Lazy loading may sometimes mark the website's ranking on search engines due to inappropriate indexing of the uploaded content.

How to Install Lazy Loading Components in the React

As the front-end application's bundle size increased, developers or designers started to investigate to find more active ways to load the bundles to the client quicker. Code-splitting and lazy loading are two methods for dramatically reducing the initial loading time for clients.

Strategies or Approaches to Split Your JavaScript JS Codes

- Route base splitting

- Components base splitting

- Library base splitting

Four distinct libraries are studied in order to perform these code splitting and slow loading methodologies. Let us go through the libraries one by one.

```
custom-component.js will use in further examples
/* custom-compnent.js */
import React, { useEffect } from "react";
const CustomComponent = ({ label }) => {
 useEffect(() => {
  console.log(`${label} created`);
  return () => console.log(`${label} destroyed`);
 }, []);
return <div>{label}</div>;
};
export default CustomComponent;
```

React.lazy

The new function in react allows you to load react components lazily through code piercing without help from any additional libraries. Lazy loading is rendering only-needed or critical user interface items first, and then gently opening the non-critical items later. It is now fully united into the core react library itself. We previously used *react-loadable* to achieve this, but now we have to use *react.lazy()* in the react core.

In version 16.6, React has built-in support for lazy loading components and React.lazy function takes the promise-based function and returns it.

Export your components defaulting (here our CustomComponent). That library doesn't supports named exports yet.

```
Calling the const LazyLoadedComponent = React.lazy(()
=> import('./custom-component.js')
Use <LazyLoadedComponent />
```

In the below example, I used the promise and a timeout to show loading effect:

```
<Suspense /> is a react component that contains a
fallback prop that accepts any other react component.
import React, { Suspense } from "react";
import ReactDOM from "react-dom";
/* wait 100 ms to render component */
const CustomComponent = React.lazy(
  () =>
  new Promise((resolve, reject) =>
   setTimeout(() => resolve(import("./custom-
                        component")), 100)
  )
);
/* wait 500 ms to render component */
const CustomComponent-1 = React.lazy(
  () =>
  new Promise((resolve, reject) =>
   setTimeout(() => resolve(import("./custom-
                        component")), 5500)
  )
);
function App() {
 return (
  <>
```

```
    <Suspense fallback={<div>Loading</div>}>
        <CustomComponent label="Component 2" />
        <CustomComponent2 label="Component 3" />
    </Suspense>
  </>
);
}
```

Wrapping all your custom (user-defined) components into one suspense as the above example will cause your user interface to show a loading indicator until the longest time to upload a component to be uploaded. In the above example, Component 2 will be created but won't be shown until Component 3 is loaded.

You may find a functional example of codes and a box here.

To get around this, wrap your lazy-loaded components with several Suspense /> components.

```
<>
  <Suspense fallback={<div>Loading</div>}>
    <CustomComponent label="Component a" />
  </Suspense>
  <Suspense fallback={<div>Loading</div>}>
    <CustomComponent2 label="Component b" />
  </Suspense>
</>
```

A working example on codes and box can be found here:

```
/* route base splitting */
const DashboardPage = React.lazy(() => import('../
pages/dashboard'));
const SettingsPage = React.lazy(() => import('../
pages/settings'));
<Route>
  <DashboardPage />
  <SettingsPage />
</Route>
```

react-loadable

react-loadable has a huge amount of features or attributes from SSR to custom rendering. Its usage is similar to @loadable/components with extra attributes.

- What it offers you,

- Built in delay, timeout attributes

- Custom rendering component instead of imported one

- SSR

- Prefetching

```
import Loadable from "react-loadable";
const CustomComponent1 = Loadable({
 loader: () =>
  new Promise((resolve, reject) => {
   setTimeout(() => resolve(import("./custom-
                            component")), 2000);
  }),
 loading: ({ pastDelay }) => (pastDelay ?
          <div>Loading...</div> : null),
 delay: 50
});
const CustomComponent2 = Loadable({
 loader: () =>
  new Promise((resolve, reject) => {
   setTimeout(() => resolve(import("./custom-
                            component")), 5000);
  }),
 loading: () => <div>Loading...</div>
});
const ErrorCustomComponent = Loadable({
 loader: () =>
  new Promise((resolve, reject) => {
   setTimeout(() => reject(import("./custom-
                            component")), 200);
  }),
 loading: ({ error }) =>
  !error ? <div>Loading...</div> : <div>Component
couldn't be loaded!</div>
});
const TimeoutComponent = Loadable({
 loader: () =>
  new Promise((resolve, reject) => {
   setTimeout(() => resolve(import("./custom-
                            component")), 2000);
```

```
  }),
 loading: ({ timedOut }) =>
  timedOut ? <div>Taking too long...</div> :
                             <div>Loading...</div>,
 timeout: 50
});
function App() {
 return (
  <>
   <CustomComponent label="Component 1" />
   <CustomComponent2 label="Component 2" />
   <ErrorCustomComponent label="Component 3" />
   <TimeoutComponent label="Component 4" />
  </>
 );
}
```

react-loadable-visibility

react-loadable-visibility is a wrapper component built or created on react-loadable and @loadable/component libraries to load the components when they are on view-port. It does with InterSectionObserver API(Application Programming Interface). It has a polyfill, but the author of that library has some misconceptions about its concert.

- What does this library provide you,

- Lazy load your components if they are present on view-port at the screen.

- Simple to use with using only the loadableVisibility function.

- You can still use the react-loadable & @loadable/component configuration

- Meaningful if your page is too long

```
import loadableVisibility from "react-loadable-visi
bility/loadable-components";
const LoadableComponent = loadableVisibility(() =>
                  import("./custom-component"), {
 fallback: () => <div>Loading...</div>
});
```

```
export default function App() {
 return <LoadableComponent />;
}
```

Let's continue with a look at our existing routes:

```
import React from 'react';
import { BrowserRouter as Router, Route, Switch } from
"react-router-dom";
import Home from './Home';
import Contact from './Contact';
import Products from './Products';

const home = () => import('./Home/index');
const contact = () => import('./Contact/index');

const Products = () => (
 <div>Products</div>
);

const Main = () => (
 <Router>
  <Switch>
   <Route path='/' exact={true} component={Home} /> } />
   <Route path='/' exact={true} component={Contact}
                                    /> } />
   <Route path='/' exact={true} component={Products}
                                    /> } />
  </Switch>
 </Router>
);

export default Main;
```

Prerequisites

To follow this part, you will need the following:

- The latest Node version must install

- create-react-app tool

npm install -g create-react-app
General instructions are:

- We will perform the lazy loading with React suspense and without it.

- First of all, create the application using npm create-react-app:

npm create-react-app my-app
Now run the application by running the following command or instruction in the project directory root.

npm start
The default react application will run at http://localhost:3000
   Let the directory structures be

```
|
|-src
|                              |-components
|                              | |-Admin.js
|                              | |-Customer.js
|                              | |-Home.js
|                              |-app.js
|-index.js
```

App would first render app.js, which will have an input value, and then send the input received as props to Home, which will then render Home .js. We will render either the Admin or the Customer based on the props obtained.

Using React Suspense (React 16.6+)

From React 16.6+, react added the React Suspense which performs lazy loading.

In our Home.js, we will do a lazy load Admin and Customer

```
import React, { Suspense } from "react";
const Customer = React.lazy(() => import("./Customer.
                                          js"));
const Admin = React.lazy(() => import("./Admin.js"));
//Instead of regular import statements and we will use
          the above method for lazy loading
```

```
export default (props) => {
if (props.user === "admin") {
return (
// fallback component is rendered until the main
                            component is loaded
<Suspense fallback={<div>Loading</div>}>
<Admin />
</Suspense>
);
} else if (props.user === "customer") {
return (
<Suspense fallback={<div>Loading</div>}>
<Customer />
</Suspense>
);
} else {
return <div> Invalid User </div>;
}
};
```

Without React Suspense

If you are using a React version older than 16.6, you will not be able to use the Suspense component. It is better to utilize Suspense and upgrade to the newest version. If you are unable to update yet and still want this feature, you can construct your own React Suspense component. Higher Order Component will be used by me (HOC).

```
Our HOC (lazyLoader.js)

const lazyLoader = (importComp) => {
return class extends React.Component {
state: {
component: null; //initializing-state
};

//loading component and setting it to state
componentDidMount() {
importComp().then((comp) => setState({ component:
comp.default }));
}
```

```
//rendering the component
render() {
const C = this.state.component;
return C ? <C {...this.props} /> : null;
}
};
};
export default lazyLoader;
Our calling component, in this, Home.js

import React from "react";
import { lazyLoader } from "./lazyLoader";

const Customer = lazyLoader(() => import("./Customer.
                                              js"));
const Admin = lazyLoader(() => import("./Admin.js"));

//Instead of the regular import statements, we will
use the above approach for lazy loading

export default (props) => {
if (props.user === "admin") {
return <Admin />;
} else if (props.user === "customer") {
return <Customer />;
} else {
return <div> Invalid User </div>;
}
};
```

If you require the fallback feature, you may modify HOC's render method, which now returns null. You may return your backup component instead of null, and it can be provided as props.

Now our HOC would look like this:

```
const lazyLoader = (importComp, fallback) => {
return class extends React.Component {
state = {
component: null, //initializing-state
};

//loading component and setting it to state
componentDidMount() {
```

```
importComp().then((comp) => setState({ component:
comp.default }));
}

//rendering the component
render() {
const C = this.state.component;
return C ? (
<C {...this.props} />
) : fallback ? (
fallback
) : (
<div>loading</div>
);
// If a component is not loaded, then return a
fallback component; if fallback is not provided, then
use default loading
}
};
};
export default lazyLoader;
```

CHAPTER 7

Advanced Tools

IN THIS CHAPTER

➤ Advanced tools

➤ Context API

➤ Hooks

➤ Render props

CONTEXT API

Context makes available a way to pass data through the component hierarchy without having to pass props down manually at each and every level. Data is passed from top-down (i.e., parent to child) via props in this typical React application, but such usage might be problematic for particular sorts of props (e.g., locale choice, user interface themes) that are required by multiple components within an application. Context allows you to communicate data like this across components without having to send a prop through every level of the tree directly.

What Is React's Context API (Application Programming Interface)?

The React Context API (Application Programming Interface) is a way for a React app to functionally define global(extern) variables that can be passed through. This is another way to "prop drilling" from different generations: grandparent to child to parent, and so on. With the use of Redux, Context is also approved as an easier, lighter approach for state

DOI: 10.1201/9781003309369-7

management. Context API is a (type of) new attribute added in React version 16.3 that let you distribute states through the entire app (or any part of it) lightly and easily.

React Context API: How Does It Work?

React.createContext() is the syntax that you required. It returns a consumer and a provider. The provider works as a module that, as its name suggests, provides the states to its children through the entire app and will hold the "store" and be the parent of all the modules that might require that store. The component that consumes and uses the state is termed Consumers.

Context API Will Replace Redux?

No. Well, it's not complete. The concept of Redux is efficient and came perfectly to answer the requirements for the management of the state. Actually, it answered the need for this concept so clearly that it came to be known that you can't be a real React developer/tester if you don't know your way around the Redux. However, Redux has its demerits, and due to this, it's important to know about the Context API gives us which Redux doesn't:

- **Simplicity**: While using redux people tend to manage almost all of their states in redux and there arise two situations:

  1. **Overhead**: What is the need to create/update 3 files, just to add one small feature?

  2. **Data Binding**: One of the significant merits of React's one-way data binding is that it's easy to understand and manage – a component passes state to its child component. Using Redux takes it away from us.

- With the use of Context API, we can define several unrelated contexts (stores) and use each in its appropriate place in the app.

How to Use Context API?

"I've been convinced, and now I want to incorporate Context API in my application," you may be thinking. First, make sure you need it. It has been found that most people use shared/distributed states across nested modules instead of passing them as props. And if you do need it, you must follow the following few steps:

Create the folder under your application root named as
    contexts (not necessary but as convention).
Create a file named as <your context_name>Context.js,
    e.g., userContext.js.
Import and create a context like the following:
import React, { createContext } from "react";
const UserContext = createContext();

- Create a component/module that will wrap the provider named Provider, e.g., UserProvider

Example using React Hooks

```
const UserProvider = ({ children }) => {
const [name, setName] = useState("John Doe");
const [age, setAge] = useState(1);
const happyBirthday = () => setAge(age + 1);
return (
<UserContext.Provider value={{ name, age,
                                happyBirthday }}>
{children}
</UserContext.Provider>
);
};
```

Create a higher order component/module to consume the context named: with, e.g., withUser.

Example using React Hooks

```
const withUser = (Child) => (props) => (<UserContext.
                                Consumer>
{(context) => <Child {...props} {...context} />}
{/* Another option is: {context => <Child {...props}
                        context={context}/>}*/}
</UserContext.Consumer>

);
```

The difference between these two options is that if you want the context to be a single nested property with this name, you must explode it to its properties (which in my opinion is more convenient).

```
Finally export them:
export { UserProvider, withUser };
And use them however you like.
For example:
ReactDOM.render(
<UserProvider>
<App />
</UserProvider>,
document.getElementById("root")
);
export default withUser (LoginForm);
```

You'll also be able to notice that I used the new "Hooks" feature that is shipped with React since version 16.8 to make it even neater and easier to create contexts.

Building/Designing an App Using Provider Pattern and Context API

1. **Explaining the Different Parts of the Application**: In this example, we intend to change the theme and perform translation based on selected language.

    We have the following components:

```
<LanguageSelection/> - Has a label "Select Language"
and a drop-down that has a list of languages.<ThemeCo
ntainer/> - Has a label "Change Theme," theme type,
and a toggle button.
<Content/> - Simply shows the content "Hello world!!"
```

We have three languages – English, French, and Spanish. The text on the screen should change to the respective language basis of your selection.

There are two themes, light and dark – you can toggle it using the button. It will also show the selected theme.

2. **Document Tree**: We can imagine the tree like this:

    Document Tree

    Document Tree

    The parent component is nothing but the provider which has language and theme in the state. It also has APIs(methods) to change the language and theme. Given this, all child components can consume the data and API directly.

3. <AppProvider/>

```
import React, { createContext } from "react";
import { getLocaleCode, getlocaleByCode } from "./
                                               data";
import AppContext from "./appContext";

class AppProvider extends React.Component {
state = {
 localeCodes: [],
 localeObj: null,
 theme: "light"
};

updateLocalCode = async e => {
try {
   const localeObj = await getlocaleByCode(e.target.va
                                               lue);
   this.setState({ localeObj });
} catch (err) {
   console.log(err);
}
};

updateTheme = e => {
 this.setState({ theme: e.target.checked ? "dark" :
"light" });
};

render() {
 return (
  <AppContext.Provider
   value={{
     state: this.state,
     updateLocale: this.updateLocalCode,
     updateTheme: this.updateTheme
   }}
  >
```

```
    <div className={this.state.theme}>{this.props.chil
                    dren}</div
    </AppContext.Provider>
  );
}
componentDidMount = async () => {
try {
  const localeCodes = await getLocaleCode();
  const localeObj = await getlocaleByCode();
  this.setState({ localeCodes, localeObj });
 } catch (err) {
   console.log(err);
 }
};
}
export default AppProvider;
```

As you can see, in this component, we are exposing the states "updateLocale" and "updateTheme." In the states, we have all the data which is shown in the UI, whereas "updateLocale" and "updateTheme" are the callbacks that are going to be used by the consumers. Here "updateLocale" holds the definition of the updateLocaleCode method – its job is to change the language. "updateTheme" holds the definition of the method "updateTheme" which toggles the theme to light or dark.

4. Let's quickly check the render of all three components:

    A. LanguageSelection

```
render() {
return (
  <AppContext.Consumer>
   {context => (
    <div className="haveMargin">
     <label className="labels">
      {context.state.localeObj.languageLabel}
     </label>
     <select
      value={context.state.localeObj.locale}
      onChange={context.updateLocale}
     >
      <option value="en-US">English</option>
      <option value="fr-FR">French</option>
      <option value="es-ES">Spanish</option>
```

```
      </select>
    </div>
  )}
  </AppContext.Consumer>
);
}
```

We are using render props and accessing the data using {context.state .localObj.languageLabel}. Also, on changing the selection, we invoke the callback using {context.updateLocale}.

B. ThemeContainer

```
render() {
return (
  <AppContext.Consumer>
   {context => (
    <div className="haveMargin">
     <label className="labels">
       {context.state.localeObj.themeLabel}:
     </label>
     . . . . . . . . . . .
     <label className="switch">
      <input type="checkbox" onChange={context.
                                    updateTheme} /
      <span className="slider round" />
     </label>
    </div>
   )}
  </AppContext.Consumer>
);
}
```

C. Content
```
render() {
 return (
  <AppContext.Consumer>
   {context => (
    <h2>{context.state.localeObj.content}</h2>
   )}
  </AppContext.Consumer>
);
}
```

We access the data in ThemeContainer and Content while we invoke the callback {context.updateTheme} basis by the toggle button in ThemeContainer.

API (Application Programming Interface)

The syntax to create "React.createContext"const UserContext = React.createContext(default Value);Creating a Context Object

When React displays a component/module that subscribes to this Context method, it will read the current context value from the Provider that is the closest match above it in the hierarchy.

The argument is the default value only when a component/function does not have a matching Provider above it in the hierarchy. This default value can be very helpful for testing components in an isolated way without wrapping them. *Note:* To pass undefined as a Provider value does not cause consuming components to use defaultValue.

Context.Provider

```
The syntax for context provider "<MyContext.Provider
value={/* some value */}>
"
```

Each Context object assigns a Provider React component that allows it to consume components that subscribe to context changes/alters.

The Provider components accept a value prop to be passed into the consuming components that are an heir of this Provider. A single Provider can be linked to several customers. Providers can be nested to override/overwrite values deeper within the mesh.

Each and every consumer that is descendants of a Provider will rerender whenever the Provider's value prop alters. The propagation/flow from Provider to its descendant consumers (including .contextType and useContext) is not subject to the shouldComponentUpdate method/function, so the consumer is likely to update even when an ancestor/previous component skips an update(modified).

Changes are determined by comparing old values to the new ones using the same algorithm as Object.is.

Note: The way modifications are determined can cause some issues/errors while passing objects as values.

Class.contextType

```
class MyClass extends React.Component {
 componentDidMount() {
  let value1 = this.context;
  //* performing a side-effect at mount using the
                             value of MyContext *//
 }
 componentDidUpdate() {
  let value1 = this.context ;
  /* ...... */
 }
 componentWillUnmount() {
  let value1 = this.context;
  /* ... */
 }
 render() {
  let value1 = this.context;
  /* render something that based on the value of
                          MyContext class */
 }
}
MyClass.contextType = MyContext;
```

This contextType feature on a class can be assigned to as a Context object designed by React.createContext(). Using these features allows you to consume the nearest current/updated value of that Context type with the use this.context class. You can reference these features in any of the lifecycle methods, including the render function/method.

Note: This API only allows you to subscribe to a single context; if you need to read more than one, see Consuming Multiple/Several Contexts.

If anyone is using the experimental public class fields syntax, one can use a static class field to initialize your contextType.

```
class MyClass extends React.Component {
 static contextType = UserContext;
 render() {
  let value1 = this.context;
  /* render something based on the value */
 }
```

```
}
Context.Consumer
The syntax of <MyContext.Consumer>
{value1 => /* render something based on the context
                value */}
</MyContext.Consumer>
```

A React component that subscribes to context modified: Using this component allows you to subscribe to a context within the function components.

Need a function as a child function: This function takes and returns the current context values to a React node. The value parameter provided to the function will be the value prop of the nearest Provider in the mesh for this context. If there is no Provider for the context above, the value argument will equal the defaultValue that was passed to createContext().

Note: See render props for more information about the function of a child's pattern.

Context.displayName

```
A displayName string attribute is available on the
Context object. This string is used by React DevTools
to determine what to show for the context.
```

For example, the following component will appear as MyDisplayName in the DevTools:

```
const MyContext = React.createContext(/* some value */);
MyContext.displayName = 'MyDisplayName';

<MyContext.Provider> // "MyDisplayName.Provider" in
                        DevTools
<MyContext.Consumer> // "MyDisplayName.Consumer" in
                        DevTools
```

INTRODUCTION TO HOOKS

Hooks are introduced in the version of React 16.8(a JavaScript library for user interface). Hooks are generally used as it allows you to use state and other React features without creating a class for it. It doesn't work inside classes.

It allows using functional components of the lifecycle, states, pure components, etc.

React also provides a few built-in Hooks like useState, useEffect etc., whereas you can also create hooks on your own.

Hooks allows you to reuse stateful logic concepts without changing your component sequence. This makes it easy to manipulate and share Hooks among many components or among the community. Before moving ahead, note that you can try Hooks in a few components without rewriting any existing code.

Hooks allow you to break into a different component of other several smaller function-based figures on what the pieces have been mapped (such as setting a subscription or detecting the data), despite making a split based on lifecycle methods. You can also choose from managing the component's initial state with a reducer to make it more predictable.

State Hook

It is a built-in Hook (useState) that is used to create a React state for the functional components. This hook has been called inside the function component to add some local state to it. It lets you build your own Hooks to reuse stateful behavior between different functional component units. Now we will go through the built-in hooks first.

This example renders a counter. Whenever the button is clicked, it increases the value.

```
import React, { useState } from 'react';
function Exmp1() {
 // Declaring a new state variable, which called as
              "count"
 const [count, set_Count] = useState(0);
 return (
  <div>
   <p>You clicked {count} times</p>
   <button onClick={() => set_Count(count + 1)}>
    Click it
   </button>
  </div>
 );
}
```

Here, useState is a Hook. In a function called Exmp1, we declare a new state variable which we called "count." It is called inside a function component/module to provide some local/initial state to it. In the above example, it is 0 because the counter is set to zero, so at every click on the button, the counter increases the value by 1. You can call this function Exmp1 from an event handler or somewhere else.

Declaring Multiple State Variables

```
function ExampleWithStates() {
  // Declare multiple state variables!
  const [age, set_Age] = useState(42);
  const [fruit, set_Fruit] = useState('banana');
  const [todos, set_Todos] = useState([{ text: 'Learn
        Hooks and React' }]);
  // ...
}
```

Effect Hook

It is also a type of built-in Hook (useEffect), it tells the React that your component needs to do something after render and also adds the ability to perform side effects from a function component whenever there are subsequent renders. Effects are declared inside (the function or main) component to have access to its props and state. It did the same as every subsequent render –

```
componentDidMount,
 componentDidUpdate,
 componentWillUnmount
```

Example:
```
import React, { useState, useEffect } from 'react';

function Friend_Status(props) {
  const [isOnline, set_Is_Online] = useState(null);

  function handleStatusChange(status) {
   setIsOnline(status._is_Online);
  }
```

```
useEffect(() => {
  ChatAPI.subscribeToFriendStatus(props.friend.id,
                              handleStatusChange);
  return () => {
    ChatAPI.unsubscribeFromFriendStatus(props.friend
                      .id, handleStatusChange);
  };
});

if (isOnline === null) {
  return 'Loading...';
}
  return isOnline ? 'Online' : 'Offline';
}
```

Here we create a new state where we update the value in the ChatAPI: whether it is online or offline, the state is set to null in the function called FriendStatus(props).

Hooks are the functions, so in the useEffect hook, we passed arguments as a function that updates the values after every subsequent renders.

Rules of Hooks

Hooks(React) are JavaScript functions, but there are two additional rules imposed :

1. Only call Hooks at the top level. Do not call Hooks into the loops, conditions, or nested functions.

2. Only call Hooks from React function components. Don't call Hooks from regular JavaScript functions.

BUILDING YOUR OWN(CUSTOM) HOOKS

Sometimes, we need to reuse some stateful logic between components, so we define our own hook called Custom Hooks. It allows you to do this, but without the addition of more components.

A custom Hook is a JavaScript function whose name starts with the "use" keyword.

For example, useFriend_Status below is our first custom hook.

```
import React, { useState, useEffect } from 'react';

function useFriendStatus(friendID) { const [isOnline,
setIsOnline] = useState('/0');
```

```
function handleStatusChange(status) {
 setIsOnline(status.isOnline);
}

useEffect(() => {

ChatAPI.subscribeToFriendStatus(friendID,
                                handleStatusChange);
 return () => {
  ChatAPI.unsubscribeFromFriendStatus(friendID,
                                handleStatusChange);
 };
});

return isOnline;

}
```

Our useFriendStatus hook is to update us on a friend's status. It takes FriendID as an argument and returns the value as online or offline.

REACT.JS RENDER PROPS

The Render Props is a technique/method in ReactJS for distributing codes between React components using a prop whose value is a function/method. Child function takes render props as a function and calls it instead of executing its own render logic. To summarize, if we give a function from the parent component to the child component as a render prop, the child component calls that function instead of creating its own logic.

Creating a React App and Downloading a Module

Step 1: Use the following command to create a React application:

foldername

npx create-react-app

Step 2: After creating project folder, i.e., foldername, use the following command to move to it:

```
cd foldername
```

The term "render prop" refers to a method for sharing codes between React components/module using the prop whose value is a function.

Instead of creating its own render logic, a component with a render prop accepts a function that yields a React element and calls it.

```
<DataProvider render={data => (

<h1>Hello {data.target}</h1>

)}/>
```

React Router, Downshift, and Formik are among the libraries that make use of render props.

FOR CROSS-CUTTING ISSUES, USE RENDER PROPS.

Components are a basic unit of code reuse in React, but it is not always clear how to share the states or actions encapsulated by one component with the other components that require the same state.

Now consider an example, the following component tracks the mouse position in a web app:

```
class MouseTracker extends React.Component {
  constructor(props) {
   super(props);
   this.handleMouseMove = this.handleMouseMove.b
                            ind(this);
   this.state = { x: 0, y: 0 };
  }

  handleMouseMove(event) {
   this.setState({
    x: event.clientX,
    y: event.clientY
   });
  }

  render() {
   return (
    <div style={{ height: '101vh' }} onMouseMove={this.
                            handleMouseMove}>
     <h1>Move the mouse around it! </h1>
     <p>The current mouse position ({this.state.x},
                            {this.state.y})</p>
    </div>
   );
  }
}
```

As a cursor moves around the screen, the component displays the (x, y) coordinates in a <p>.

Now the question is: How do we reuse this behavior in the other component? However, if another component requires information about the cursor location, can we encapsulate that behavior so that it can be readily distributed with that component?

Because elements are the fundamental unit of code reuse in React, let's modify the code to use <Mouse> component that encapsulates the behavior we need to reuse elsewhere.

```
// The <Mouse> component encapsulates the behavior we
                            need...
class Mouse extends React.Component {
 constructor(props) {
  super(props);
  this.handleMouseMove = this.handleMouseMove.b
                            ind(this);
  this.state = { x: 0, y: 0 };
 }

 handleMouseMove(event) {
  this.setState({
   x: event.clientX,
   y: event.clientY
  });
 }

 render() {
  return (
   <div style={{ height: '101vh' }} onMouseMove={this.
            handleMouseMove}>

    {/* ...but how could we render something other
                    than a <p>? */}
    <p>The current(new) mouse position is ({this
                    .state.x}, {this.state.y})</p>
   </div>
  );
 }
}
```

```
class MouseTracker extends React.Component {
 render() {
  return (
   <>
    <h1>Move the mouse around!</h1>
    <Mouse />
   </>
  );
 }
}
```

The <Mouse> component encapsulates all behaviors related to listening for mousemove events and storing the (x, y) position of the cursor, but it is not yet truly reusable.

Let us consider an example that we have a <Cat> component that renders the image of a cat chasing a mouse around the screen. We must use a <Cat mouse={{ x, y }}> prop to tell the component about the coordinates of the mouse to know about the position of the image on the screen.

As a first render, you might try rendering the <Cat> *inside <Mouse>'s render method*, like this:

```
class Cat extends React.Component {
 render() {
  const mouse = this.props.mouse;
  return (
   <img src="/cat.jpeg" style={{ position:
        'absolute', left: mouse.x, top: mouse.y }} />
  );
 }
}
```

```
class MouseWithCat extends React.Component {
 constructor(props) {
  super(props);
  this.handleMouseMove = this.handleMouseMove.b
                         ind(this);
  this.state = { x: 0, y: 0 };
 }
```

```
handleMouseMove(event) {
 this.setState({
  x: event.clientX,
  y: event.clientY
 });
}

render() {
 return (
  <div style={{ height: '100vh' }} onMouseMove={this.
                                    handleMouseMove}>

   {/*
    We could just swap out the <p> for a <Cat> here
                                    ... but then
    we would need to create a separate
                     <MouseWithSomethingElse>
    component each time we need to use it, so
                          <MouseWithCat>
    isn't reusable yet.
   */}
   <Cat mouse={this.state} />
  </div>
 );
 }
}

class MouseTracker extends React.Component {
 render() {
  return (
   <div>
    <h1>Move the mouse around!</h1>
    <MouseWithCat />
   </div>
  );
 }
}
```

This approach will work for our specifying use case, but we have not achieved the objective of truly encapsulating the manner in a reusable way. Each time we need the mouse position for different use cases, we have to design a new component (i.e., essentially the other <MouseWithCat>) that renders something specifically for that use case.

This is when the render prop comes into play: rather than hard-coding a Cat> within a Mouse> component and essentially modifying its displayed output, we may supply a function prop that Mouse> uses to select what to render – a render prop dynamically.

```
class Cat extends React.Component {
 render() {
  const mouse = this.props.mouse;
  return (
   <img src="/cat.jpeg" style={{ position:
       'absolute', left: mouse.x, top: mouse.y }} />
  );
 }
}

class Mouse extends React.Component {
 constructor(props) {
  super(props);
  this.handleMouseMove = this.handleMouseMove.b
                        ind(this);
  this.state = { x: 0, y: 0 };
 }
 handleMouseMove(event) {
  this.setState({
   x: event.clientX,
   y: event.clientY
  });
 }
 render() {
  return (
   <div style={{ height: '101vh' }} onMouseMove={this.
                                   handleMouseMove}>

   {/*
    Despite providing a static representation of what
                      <Mouse> renders,
    use the 'render' prop to clarify what to render
          dynamically.
    */}
    {this.props.render(this.state)}
   </div>
  );
 }
}
```

```
class MouseTracker extends React.Component {
render() {
  return (
   <div>
    <h1>Move the mouse around!</h1>
    <Mouse render={mouse => (
      <Cat mouse={mouse} />
    )}/>
   </div>
  );
 }
}
```

Now, despite productively cloning the <Mouse> components and hard-coding something else in its render method to resolve for a specific use case, we provide a render prop that <Mouse> can use to understand what it renders firmly.

The render prop is a function prop that the component uses to know what to render.

This technique/method makes the behavior that we need to distribute extremely portable. To get this behavior, render a <Mouse> with a render prop that informs what to render with the cursor's current (x, y).

One interesting thing to know about render props is that you can implement the most higher order components (HOC) using a regular component with the render prop. Consider an example: if you would prefer to have the withMouse HOC instead of a <Mouse> components, you could easily define one using a regular <Mouse> with the render prop:

```
// If you really need a HOC for some reason, you can
// create one using a regular components with a render
prop!
function withMouse(Component) {
 return class extends React.Component {
  render() {
   return (
    <Mouse render={mouse => (
      <Component {...this.props} mouse={mouse} />
    )}/>
   );
  }
 }
}
```

Using a render prop allows you to employ either pattern.

OTHER THAN RENDERING PROPS

It's crucial to realize that because the pattern is called *render props*, you don't have to utilize a render prop to use it. In fact, a render prop is any prop that is a function that a component/method uses to determine what to render.

Although the above examples are used to render, we could just as easily use the children's prop!

```
<Mouse children={mouse => (
 <p>The Mouse position is_ {mouse.x}, {mouse.y}</p>
)}/>
```

And remember that the children prop doesn't require to be named in the list of "attributes" in your JSX element. In spite of that, you can put it directly *inside* the element!

```
<Mouse>
 {mouse => (
  <p>The Mouse position is_ {mouse.x}, {mouse.y}</p>
 )}
</Mouse>
```

You'll see this technique/method used in the *react-motion* API.

Because this technique/method is a little odd, you should definitely clearly indicate in your propTypes that child should be a function when creating an API like this.

```
Mouse.propTypes = {
 children: PropTypes.func.isRequired
};
```

CAVEATS

Be attentive while using Render Props with React.PureComponent

with the use of a render, prop can restrict the advantage that comes from the use of React.PureComponent if you define the function inside a render method. This is why the shallow prop comparison will always return false for new props, and each render, in this case, will generate a fresh value for the render prop.

For example, if Mouse were to extend React, ongoing with our <Mouse> component/module from above.PureComponent instead of React.Component, our example would look like this:

```
class Mouse extends React.PureComponent {
  // identical implementation like above...
}

class MouseTracker extend React.Component {
render() {
  return (
   <div>
    <h1>Move the mouse around!</h1>

    {/*
      This is bad! The value of the 'render' prop will
      be different on each render.
    */}
    <Mouse render={mouse => (
      <Cat mouse={mouse} />
    )}/>
   </div>
  );
 }
}
```

In this example, every time <MouseTracker> renders, it generates a new function as the values of the <Mouse render> prop, thus negating the effects of <Mouse> extending React.PureComponent in the initial place!

To get around this problem, you can sometimes define the prop as an instance method, like the following:

```
class MouseTracker extends React.Component {
  // Defined as an instance technique, 'this.
                        renderTheCat' every time
  // refers to *same* function/method when we use it in
                        render
  renderTheCat(mouse) {
   return <Cat mouse={mouse} />;
  }
```

```
render() {
  return (
    <div>
      <h1>Move the mouse around!</h1>
      <Mouse render={this.renderTheCat} />
    </div>
  );
}
}
```

If you cannot define the prop statically (e.g., because you need to close over the component's props and/or state) <Mouse> should extend React. Component instead.

CHAPTER 8

Testing Your Code

IN THIS CHAPTER

➤ Testing

➤ Jest

➤ Nock

➤ react-testing-library

You can check React components in the same way that you would test any JavaScript code.

There are some ways to test React components. Broadly, they are divided into two categories:

1. **Rendering component trees** in a basic test environment and asserting their output.

2. **Running a complete app** in a genuine browser environment (also known as "end-to-end" tests).

This documentation unit focuses on challenging approaches for the first event. While full end-to-end tests can be very valuable to prevent regressions to significant workflows, such tests are not concerned with the React components in particular and are out of the scope of this section.

DOI: 10.1201/9781003309369-8

TRADE-OFFS

When selecting testing tools, it is worth noting a few trade-offs:

- **Iteration speed vs. realistic environment:** Some tools offer a very quick response loop between making a modification and seeing the result but do not model the browser behavior precisely. Other tools might use an actual browser environment, but reduce the iteration speed and are flakier on a continuous combination server.

- **How much to mock:** With components, the difference between a "unit" and an "integration" test can be blurry. If you're testing a form, would it experiment and also test the buttons inside of it? Or should a button component have its own test suite? Should refactoring a button ever break the form test?

Different responses may work for different teams and products.

Recommended Tools

Jest is a JavaScript assessment runner that allows you to access the DOM via jsdom. While jsdom is only an estimate of how the browser works, it is frequently good and sufficient for testing the React components. Jest has a fast repetition rate mixed with sophisticated features like mocking modules and timers to give you more control over how the code executes.

React Testing Library is a set of helpers that allows you to test React components without relying on their execution details. This method makes refactoring a breeze and also pushes you toward the best performance for availability. Even though it doesn't provide a way to "shallowly" render a module without its children, a test runner like Jest allows you to do this by *mocking*.

In this chapter, I'm going to introduce you to a React testing tool named Jest, along with the popular public library Enzyme, which is considered to test React components. I'll announce to you Jest testing methods, including running tests, testing React components, snapshot testing, and mocking. If you are new to testing and inquisitive about how to get going, you will find this chapter helpful because we will start with an outline for testing. By the end, you will be up and running, testing React apps using Jest and Enzyme. You should be acquainted with React in order to follow this chapter.

A BRIEF INTRODUCTION TO TESTING

Challenging is a line-by-line review of how your code will implement. A suite of tests for an application contains various bits of code to authenticate whether an app is executing effectively and without fault. When codes are updated, testing comes in helpful as well. After upgrading a piece of code, you may run a test to ensure that the update does not damage existing app functionality.

Why Test?

It is good to understand why we are doing something before doing it. So, why test, and what is its persistence?

The first resolution of testing is to avoid regression. Regression is the reappearance of an error that had formerly been fixed. It is a kind of feature stop effective as intended after a certain incident occurs.

Testing confirms the functionality of composite components and modular apps.

Testing is needed for the effective performance of a software app or product.

Testing makes an app more vigorous and less prone to error. It is a way to authenticate that your code does what you want it to do and that your app works as projected for your users.

Let us go over the types of testing and what they do.

Unit Test

In this kind of test, a specific unit or component of the software is tested. A unit might be an individual function, component, method, procedure, module, or object. A unit test separates a section of codes and verifies its precision, in order to confirm that each unit of the software's code accomplishes as probable.

In unit testing, individual processor functions are verified to guarantee that they are operating appropriately, and that all components are tested independently. For instance, testing a function whether an announcement or a loop in a program is functioning appropriately would fall under the scope of unit testing.

Component Test

Component testing authenticates the functionality of a specific part of an app. Tests are executed on each component in isolation from the other components. Generally, React apps are made up of several components, so component challenging deals with testing these components exclusively.

For example, consider a website that has dissimilar web pages with several components. Each component will have its own subcomponents. Testing each module without considering addition with other components is denoted as component testing.

Testing like this in React needs more sophisticated tools. So, we would require Jest and sometimes more sophisticated tools, like Enzyme, which we will deliberate on shortly later.

Snapshot Test

A snapshot test confirms that the user interface (UI) of a website app does not change unexpectedly. It records the code of a module at a certain point in time, allowing us to compare the component in one state to any other likely state it may generate.

We will study snapshot testing in a future section.

Advantages and Disadvantages of Testing

Testing is the part that is great and should be done, but it has advantages and disadvantages.

Advantages #

- It avoids unexpected deterioration.

- It permits the developer to focus on the existing task, rather than worrying about the past.

- It permits the modular construction of an application that would otherwise be too complex to build.

- It reduces the need for manual confirmation.

Disadvantages #

- You require to write more code, as well as fix and maintain.

- Non-critical test disappointments might cause the app to be excluded in terms of continuous incorporation.

INTRODUCTION TO JEST

Jest is a pleasant JavaScript challenging framework with a focus on effortlessness. It can be installed or set up with npm or Yarn. Jest fit into a broader class of utilities known as test runners. It works great for React apps, but it also works great for external React apps.

The Enzyme is a package for testing React applications. It is intended to test components and makes it possible to build declarations that imitate actions to validate whether the UI is functioning properly.

Jest and Enzyme accompany each other well, so in this piece, we will be using both of them.

Process of Running a Test with Jest

In this part, we will be installing Jest and writing tests for it. If you are new to ReactJS, then I acclaim using Create React App, for the reason that it is ready for use and ships with Jest.

```
npm init react-app my-app
```

We require to install Enzyme ****and enzyme-adapter-react-16 with react-test-renderer (the number should be based on the variety of React you are using).

```
npm install --save-dev enzyme enzyme-adapter-react-16
react-test-renderer
```

Note that we have created our project with both Jest and Enzyme, we need to create a setupTest.js file in the project's src folder. This is how the file would look:

```
import { configure } from "enzyme";
import Adapter from "enzyme-adapter-react-16";
configure({ adapter: new Adapter() });
```

This significant Enzyme sets up the connecter to run our tests.

Before continuing, let us learn some basics. Some key belongings have been used a lot in this chapter, and you will need to clear them or test them. You would pass a function or method to this technique, and the test runner would perform that determination as a block of tests.

- **Describe**: This elective method is for alliance any number of it or test declarations.

- **Expect**: This is the disorder that the test requires to pass. It differentiates the received parameter from the matcher and it also provides you admittance to a number of matches that allow you to validate dissimilar things. You can read more about it in this section.

- **Mount**: This method renders the complete DOM, including the child components of the parent component, in which we are consecutively the tests.

- **Shallow**: This renders only the specific components that we are challenging. It does not render child components. This allows us to test components in separation.

Creating a Test File

How does Jest know what is a test file and what is not? The first rule is that any file found in any directory with the name __test__ is considered to be tested. If you place a JS file in one of these directories, Jest will, for better or worse, try to run it when you call Jest. The second guideline is that Jest will look for any file with a suffix such as .spec.js or .test.js before searching the names of all folders and files in your whole repository.

Let us create our first test, for a React mini-app design for this chapter. You can make it on GitHub. Run or execute npm install to install all of the packages and libraries, and then npm start to launch the application.

Let us open App.test.js to write our first test. First, check whether our application component renders correctly and whether we have specified an output:

```
it("renders without crashing", () => {
  shallow(<App />);
});

it("renders Account header", () => {
  const wrapper = shallow(<App />);
  const welcome = <h1>Display Active Users Account
Details</h1>;
  expect(wrapper.contains(welcome)).toEqual(true);
});
```

In the above test, the first test, with shallows, checks to illustrate whether our app component renders in a correct manner without crashing, and remember that the shallow method renders only a single component, without child components.

With a Jest matcher of toEqual, the second test checks if we have the requested h1 tag output of the "Display Active User Account" in app component.

Run the Code

```
npm run test
/* OR */
npm test
```

The output in your terminal should be like this:

```
PASS src/App.test.js
√ renders without crashing (34ms)
√ renders Account header (13ms)


Test Suites: 1 passed, 1 total
Tests:    2 passed, 2 total
Snapshots:   0 total
Time:    11.239s, estimated 16s
Run all the test suites related to changed files.
```

As you can see that our test passed. It shows that we have one test suite named App.test.js, with two consecutive successful tests when the Jest ran. We will talk about snapshot testing further, and you will also get to consider an example of a failed test.

Skipping or Isolating a Test #

Skipping or isolating the test means that when Jest runs, a specific marked test is not executed.

```
it.skip("renders without crashing", () => {
  shallow(<App />);
});
```

```
it("renders Account header", () => {
 const wrapper = shallow(<App />);
 const header = <h1>Display Active Users Account
              Details</h1>;
 expect(wrapper.contains(header)).toEqual(true);
});
```

Our first test will be skipped because we have used the skip method to separate the test. So, it will not execute or make any alteration to our test when Jest runs and only the second one will execute. You can also use it .only().

It is a bit frustrating to make changes in a text file and then have to manually run the npm test again. Jest has a nice attribute called watch mode, which watches for file changes and runs tests, respectively. To run Jest in watch-mode, you can run npm test -- --watch or jest --watch and I would also recommend leaving Jest executing in the terminal window for the rest of this lesson.

Mocking Function

A mock is a convincing duplicate or look-alike of a module or object without any real inner working. It may have a tiny or small functionality, but compared to the real thing, it is a mock. Jest may generate it either manually or automatically.

Why should we mock, or do we even need to mock? Mocking decreases dependencies, or the amount of associated files that must be loaded and processed when a test is executed. Using a large number of mocks speeds up test execution.

Mock functions are sometimes known as "spies" because they allow you to spy on the behavior of a function that is directly called by another piece of code, rather than merely evaluating the output of the code.

There are two ways to mock a function: either create a mock function to use it in the test code or write a manual mock to override a module dependency.

Manual mocks are used to press out functionality with the mock data. For example, rather than accessing a remote resource, like a database or a website, you may want to make or create a manual mock that allows you to use the fake data.

We will use the mock function in the coming section.

Testing React Components #

This section will combine all of the knowledge we have acquired till now in understanding how to test the React components. Testing involves ensuring the output of a component has not unexpectedly changed to something else. Creating components in the right way is the most effective way to ensure successful testing.

One thing we may do is to verify the component's props, specifically whether or not props from one component are sent to another. Enzyme and the Jest API allow creating a mock function to simulate whether props are being passed between the components or not.

We need to pass the user-account props to the Account component from the main App component. We have to give user-account details to the Account in order to render or process the active account of the users. This is where mocking comes in use, enabling us to test our components with fake data.

Let us create a mock for the user props:

```
const user = {
  name: "Adeneye David",
  email: "davidadeneye@gmail.com",
  username: "Dave_Bautista",
};
```

We have formed a manual mock function in the test file and enclosed it around the component. Let's assume we are testing a very large database of users. Accessing the database directly from the text file is not wise. Instead, we create a mock function, which allows us to use fake data to test our component.

```
describe("", () => {
  it("accepts user account props", () => {
    const wrapper = mount(<Account user={user} />);
    expect(wrapper.props().user).toEqual(user);
  });
  it("contains users account email", () => {
    const wrapper = mount(<Account user={user} />);
    const value = wrapper.find("p").text();
    expect(value).toEqual("david@gmail.com");
  });
});
```

We have two tests above, and we use a describe layer, which takes the component that is being tested. By mentioning the values and props that we expect to be passed by the test, we are able to proceed further.

In our first test, we see if the props we gave to the mounted component match the mock props we produced earlier.

In the second test, we send the user props to the mounted Account components and then see whether we can discover the <p> element that correlates to what is in the Account components. When we run the test suite, you will see that the test runs successfully.

We can also test the states of our components. Let us check whether the state of the error message is equal to null:

```
it("renders correctly with no error message", () => {
  const wrapper = mount();
  expect(wrapper.state("error")).toEqual(null);
});
```

In this test, we determine whether the state of our components error or bug is equal to null, using a toEqual() matcher function. If there is a bug or error message in our application, the test will fail when executed.

In this lesson, we'll go through how to test React components using snapshot testing, which is yet another fantastic methodology or method.

Snapshot Testing

Snapshot testing captures the codes of components at a moment in the time, in order to match them to reference snapshot files saved alongside the test. It is used to keep track of modifications in an application's UI.

The actual code representation of a snapshot is a JSON file, and this JSON contains a record of what the components looked like when the snapshot was created. During a test, Jest matches the contents of this JSON file to the output of the components during the test and if they match, the test passes; if they do not, the test fails.

To change an Enzyme wrapper to a format that is just with Jest snapshot testing, we have to install enzyme-to-json:

```
npm install --save-dev enzyme-to-JSON
```

Let us write our snapshot test and run it for the first time; a snapshot of that component's code will compose and be saved in a new __snapshots__ folder in the src directory.

```
it("renders correctly", () => {
 const tree = shallow(<App />);
 expect(toJson(tree)).toMatchSnapshot();
});
```

When the test above executes successfully, the current user interface component will be compared to the existing one.

Now, let's run the test:

```
npm run test
```

As explained in the last section, the shallow method from the Enzyme package is used to render a single component and nothing else. It does not render child components. Rather, it gives us a clear way to separate codes and get better data when debugging. The alternative method, mount, is used to render the whole DOM, including the child component of the parent component in which the tests are being run.

Let us make some changes to our components in order to make our test fail, which will happen. To do this, let us change the <h3> tag in our components from <h3> Loading...</h3> to <h3>Fetching the Users...</h3>. When the test executes, this is what we will have in the terminal:

```
FAIL  src/App.test.js (30.696s)
 X renders correctly (44ms)

 • renders correctly
  expect(received).toMatchSnapshot()
  Snapshot name: 'renders correctly
1

  - Snapshot
  + Received

Displays the Active User's Account Details
      -    Loading...
      +    Fetching the Users...


  | it("renders correctly", ()
=> {
```

```
      |    const wrapper = shallow();
   >  |    expect(toJson(wrapper)).toMatchSnapshot();
      |                   ^    10 | });
      |
      | /* it("renders without crashing", () => {
      at Object. (src/App.test.js:9:27)
```

> 1 snapshot failed.

Execute all test suites related to changed files.

Watch Usage: Press 'w' to show more.

If we need our test to pass, we would either alter the test to its last state or update the snapshot file. In the command line, Jest provides instructions or commands on how to update the snapshot. First of all, press w in the command line to show more, and then press u to update snapshot.

> Press u to update the failing snapshots.

The test will fail if we click u to update the snapshot.

WHAT IS NOCK?

- Nock is an HTTP (hypertext markup protocol) server mocking and expectations library for the Node.js.

- Nock can be used to test a module that performs HTTP requests in an isolated way.

- Nock works by overriding Node's HTTP.request functions. Also, it overrides HTTP.ClientRequest too to cover modules or components that use it directly.

- Nock lets us avoid the mentioned challenges by intercepting external HTTP requests and enabling us to either return custom responses to test differential scenarios or store real responses as "fixtures," canned data that will return reliable responses.

Using canned data or information does come with risks, as it can go stale if not refreshed or render periodically. Without special extra tests or pinned API (Application Programming Interface) versioning, a change in the structure of the data supplied by an API may go undetected, and it is the developer's duty to ensure that policies are in place to avoid this.

In our end-to-end testing, for example, we see an example from my present company. These employ Nock fixtures since they would occasionally fail due to timeouts while running during our continuous delivery process. However, each time the developer runs these tests locally, the fixtures are immediately destroyed and regenerated, keeping them up to date.

- Nock is currently used in two chief ways:

  1. Mocking individual responses specified by the developer or designer uses Nock

  2. Recording, saving, and reusing/reusable live responses use nock.back

Either can be within individual tests and if both are used within the same test files, then the nock.back mode must be directly set, and reset, before and after use, and we will look at this in detail afterward.

Let us set up the project, add Nock, then look at nock and nock.back with some code examples.

Adding Nock

We will be creating this project that contains some simplistic functions that call a random user-created API, perfect for testing out the Nock. It uses Jest as it is a test runner and for assertions.

There are three functions to be tested in this instance: obtaining a random user, getting a random user of a certain nation, and getting a random user but falling back to the default value if failed. Other examples:

```
const getRandomUserOfNationality = n =>
 fetch(`https://random_user.me/api/?nat=${n}`)
  .then(throwNon200)
  .then(res => res.json())
  .catch(e => console.log(e));
```

As we are using the nock.back, the nock.js helper file is also used, we will look at this later.

Using "Nock"

The Nock documents explain this pretty well. Several options are available to specify the alteration of the requests, whether in the request resembles or the response returned. The two examples of this would be the response returned from the successful request, and force 500 responses to test the function's fallback options.

All that would require to be added to the existing test file to start using Nock is the const nock = require('nock'); / import nock from 'nock';.

In the first test, we use the string to compare the hostname and path, specify a reply code and body, and add our assertion to the Promise chain of our function calls. When the outgoing request from getRandomUser() is formed, it resembles the Nock interceptor we just set up, and so the reply we specify is returned.

```
it('should return a user', () => {
 nock('https://randomuser.me')
  .get('/api/')
  .reply(200, {
   results: [{ name: 'Dominic_' }],
  });
 return query
  .getRandomUser()
  .then(res => res.results[0].name)
  .then(res => expect(res).toEqual('Dominic_'));
});
```

Similarly, we mock the call with a specific nationality, so this time we use a RegExp to compare the hostname and path.

```
it('should return a user of set the nationality', ()
=> {
 nock(/random/)
  .get(/nat=gb/)
  .reply(200, {
   results: [{ nat: 'GB' }],
  });
 return query
  .getRandomUserOfNationality('gb')
  .then(res => res.results[0].nat)
  .then(res => expect(res).toEqual('GB'));
});
```

It is important to specify we are using afterAll(nock.restore) and afterEach(nock.cleanAll) to make sure interceptors do not interrupt each other.

Finally, we test 500 responses. For this we formed an additional function that returns a default value if the API call does not return any response. We will use Nock to intercept the request and mock 500 responses, and then test what function returns.

```
it('should return the default user on 500', () => {
  nock(/randomuser/)
    .get(/api/)
    .reply(500);
  return query
    .getRandomUserGuarded()
    .then(res => expect(res).
toMatchObject(defaultUser));
});
```

Being able to mock the non-200 response codes, delaying the connection, and socket timeouts is differentially useful.

Using 'nock.back'

nock.back is much used not just to intercept the HTTP request, but also to save a real response for future use, and this saved response is termed a "fixture."

In the record mode, if the named fixture is present, it will use live calls, and if it is not present, then a fixture will be created for further calls.

In this example project, only one HTTP call is being prepared per test, but nock.back fixtures can record all the outgoing calls. This is particularly useful when testing a tuff component that makes calls to several services or during end-to-end testing where a variety of calls can be made. A main merit of using fixtures is that once generated, they are fast to access, reducing the chances of timeouts. As they use real-time data, mocking the data structure is not compulsory, and any changes can be identified.

As mentioned, it is necessary to delete and refresh fixtures regularly to ensure they do not go out stale.

A present "feature" of nock.back is that when used in the same test file as standard nock interceptors, they can interrelate with each other unless any of nock.backtests are bookended per test as follows:

```
nock.back.setMode('record');
// your test
nock.back.setMode('wild');
```

This ensures that any of the following tests do not unintentionally use created fixtures. I have not done it, then, for example, the 500 responses would not be given in the previous test, as the fixture contains 200 responses.

We have to first set up a nock.js helper file and in the example, this is doing three things:

1. Setting the paths of where to save our fixtures.

2. Setting the modes to record so that we both record and use fixtures when tests are executed, rather than the default dryrun that only uses existing fixtures but does not record refreshed ones.

3. Using the after-Record option to perform some action on our fixtures to make it more human-readable.

This is then accessible in the test files using the const defaultOptions = require('./helpers/nock); / import defaultOptions from the './helpers/ nock';.

nock.back should be used with both Promises or Async/Await, examples are given of each. Here we will look at the latter.

```
it('should return a user', async () => {
  nock.back.setMode('record');
  const { nockDone } = await nock.back(
    'user-data.json',
    defaultOptions,
  );
  const userInfo = await query.getRandomUser();
  expect(userInfo).toEqual(
    expect.objectContaining({
      results: expect.any(Object),
    }),
  );
  nockDone();
  nock.back.setMode('wild');
});
```

We first mark the test as asynchronous, to permit us to use Await. We set the mode to record state. We pass in the name of the files we like to store our fixtures as, and the default-Options set in our nock.js helper to make them much human-readable. Once finished, this provides us with a nockDone function, to be called after our expectations are done.

After calling the getRandomUser(), we can now match its result with our expectation. For simplifying to demonstrate, we just assert that it will contain results, which itself contains an Object.

Later we set the mode to wild, as in this case we require to ensure the other tests do not use the fixture.

The fixtures themselves can be seen in a directory specified in the nock .js helper, and are themselves interesting to look at.

Final Thoughts

Nock provides strong tools for increasing the dependability of tests that use external services and enabling higher test coverage since tests that were previously deemed too flaky to implement may be evaluated.

As with mocks, it is the developer's obligation or duty to ensure that mocking does not go too far, and that the test may still fail due to a change in functionality, or it is useless.

React Testing Library is the testing utility tool that is built to test the actual DOM hierarchy rendered by React on the browser. The goal of the library is to let you write tests that resemble how a user would use your app. This can provide you with more confidence that your app works as intended when a real user does use it.

The library allows this by providing utility methods or techniques that will query the DOM in the same way the user would. For example, if a user finds a button to "Save" their work based on its content, the library provides the getByText() method or ideas. Later you'll learn more about the library's testing techniques.

But first, let us see an example of the React Testing Library in action.

How to Use React Testing Library

A Create React Project (or CRA)-created or designed React app already contains both the React Testing Library and Jest by default, so all you have to do is write your test code.

If you need to utilize the React Testing Library outside of a CRA project, you must manually install both the React Testing Library and Jest using NPM:

```
npm install --save-dev @testing-library/react jest
```

Installing React Testing Library and Jest

You need to install Jest because the React Testing Library only provides methods or techniques to help you to write the test scripts. So you still require a JavaScript test framework to execute the test codes.

Other test frameworks, such as Mocha or Jasmine, can be used, but I'll pick Jest because it performs well with both React and Testing Libraries.

In this section, I will create a new React application with CRA using the default template:

```
npx create-react-app react-test-example
```

Create a New React App with CRA

Once the app is created or designed, you should have an App.test.js file already generated or created inside the src/ folder. The content of the files would be as follows:

```
import { render, screen } from '@testing-library/
react';
import App from './App';

test('renders learn react link', () => {
  render(<App />);
  const linkElement = screen.getByText(/learn react/i);
  expect(linkElement).toBeInTheDocument();
});
```

Default CRA Test Code

The test code above used React Testing Library's render method or technique to virtually render the App components imported from the App.js file and appends them to the document.body node, and you can access the rendered HTML through the screen objects.

For seeing the result of the render() call, you can use the screen.debug() method:

```
import { render, screen } from '@testing-library/
react';
import App from './App';
test('renders learn react link', () => {
  render(<App />);
  screen.debug();
});
```

Debug the Element Rendered by React Testing Libraries

Then open your terminal and run npm run test command. You'll see the whole document.body tree rendered into your console:

```
<body>
 <div>
  <div class="App">
   <header class="Apsp-header">
    <img alt="logo" class="App-logo" src="logo.svg" />
    <p>
     Edit<code> src/App.js </code>and save to reload.
    </p>
    <a
     class="App-link"
     href="https://reactjs.org"
     rel="noopener noreferrer"
     target="_blank"
    >
     Learn React
    </a>
   </header>
  </div>
 </div>
</body>
```

The document's body rendered by the React Testing Library:

The screen objects also have the DOM testing techniques already bound into it. That is why the above test code could use screen.getByText() to queries the anchor <a> element by its textContent values.

Finally, the test codes will assert whether the link elements are available in the document object or not with the expected method from Jest:

```
expect(linkElement).toBeInTheDocument();
```

Ascertain whether the link element is present in the document.

Jest will fail the test if the link element is not found.

React Testing Library Methods for the Finding Elements

Most of your React test cases should use techniques for finding the element. React Testing Library gives you several methods to find elements by specific attributes or functions in addition to the getByText() method:

- **getByText()**:by its textContent values

- **getByRole()**: by its role the attribute value

- **getByLabelText()**: by its label attribute values

- **getByPlaceholderText()**: by its placeholder attribute value

- **getByAltText()**: by its alt attribute values

- **getByDisplayValue()**: by its value attributes, usually for <input> elements

- **getByTitle()**: by its title attributes value

And when these techniques are not enough, you can use the getByTestId() method, which allows you to find an element by its data-tested attribute:

```
import { render, screen } from '@testing-library/
react';
```

```
render(<div data-testid="custom-element" />);
const element = screen.getByTestId('custom-element');
Get element by data-testid value
```

But since selecting elements using data-tested attributes does not resemble how a real user would use your app, the documentation recommends you use it only as a last resort when all other methods fail to find your elements. Finding by Text, Role or Label should cover most cases.

How to Test User Designed Events with React Testing Library

Aside from finding whether elements exist in your document body, React Testing Library also helps you test user-formed events, like clicking on a button and typing values into the textbox.

The user-event library is a companion library for simulating user–browser interactions. Suppose you have button components to toggle between Light and Dark themes as follows:

```
import React, { useState } from "react";
function App() {
 const [theme, setTheme] = useState("light");
 const toggleTheme = () => {
```

```
  const nextTheme = theme === "light" ? "dark" : "light";
  setTheme(nextTheme);
 };
 return <button onClick={toggleTheme}>
   Current theme: {theme}
   </button>;
}

export default App;
```

Next, you create or form a test that finds the button and simulates a click event with the use of the userEvent.click() method, and once the button is clicked, you can assert the test is a success by inspecting whether the button element text contains "dark" or not:

```
import { render, screen } from "@testing-library/react";
import userEvent from "@testing-library/user-event";
import App from "./App";
test("Test theme button toggle", () => {
 render(<App />);
 const buttonEl = screen.getByText(/Current theme/i);
 userEvent.click(buttonEl);
 expect(buttonEl).toHaveTextContent(/dark/i);
});
```

Testing user clicks on the button and assert the contents.

And that is how you can simulate the user events with React Testing Libraries. The user-event library also has several other methods like dblClick for double-clicking an element and type for typing into a textbox. You can check out the documentation for user-event library for more info.

CHAPTER 9

Redux

IN THIS CHAPTER

- ➤ REDUX
- ➤ Redux basics
- ➤ Actions
- ➤ REducers
- ➤ Store
- ➤ Adding Redux to React
- ➤ Sagas, side effects
- ➤ Redux form

ReactJS is a flexible, declarative, and flexible JavaScript library for creating reusable user interface (UI) components. Redux is a component-based, open-source, front-end library responsible for the view layer of the application. It was created by a software engineer at Facebook, Jordan Walke. It was developed and maintained by Facebook and was then later used in its products like Instagram and WhatsApp. Facebook developed ReactJS in 2011 in its newsfeed section, but it was later released to the public or every user in May 2013.

DOI: 10.1201/9781003309369-9

Most websites, today, are built using MVC (Model View Controller) architecture. In the MVC architecture, React is the "V," which stands for view, whereas the architecture is provided by the Flux or Redux.

ReactJS application is made up of multiple or more than one component, where each component is responsible for outputting a small and reusable piece of HTML code.

These components are the heart of all React applications. All these components can be mixed with several other components to allow complex applications to be built of very simple building blocks. To populate data in the HTML DOM, ReactJS uses a virtual DOM-based technique. The virtual DOM is quick because it simply modifies individual DOM items rather than refreshing the entire DOM every time.

To create a React app, we write React components that correspond to or match various elements. These components are organized into higher-level components that comprise the application structure. Consider a form with features such as input fields, labels, or buttons. Each form element may be written as a React component, and then combined into a higher-level component, i.e., the form component itself. The form components would define the form's structure as well as the items contained inside it.

The process of passing the data all the way down and back up the tree introduces complexity that the libraries like Redux are designed to reduce. Instead of passing the data up the tree through a two-way function binding, we can dispatch actions directly from the child components to update the application state.

In this chapter, we will be looking forward to various different ways to incorporate the Redux store.

At first, we will see how the store can be used without the help of any additional framework. After this, we are going to explore react-redux, a framework that will be used to integrate a Redux store with the React component.

EXPLICITLY PASSING THE STORE

The first, and the most logical and important, way to include the store into your UI is to pass it down the component tree explicitly as the property. This strategy is straightforward and effective for tiny apps with only a few nested components.

Let's have a look at how can we incorporate the store into the color organizer. Inside the ./

index.js file, we will render an App component and pass it to the store:

```
import React from 'react'
import ReactDOM from 'react-dom'
import App from './components/App'
import storeFactory from './store'
const store = storeFactory()
const render = () =>
ReactDOM.render(
<App store{store}/>,
document.getElementById('react-container')
)
store.subscribe(render)
render()
```

This is ./index.js file. In this, we can create the store with the help of storeFactory and render the App component into the documents. When the App is rendered to the store, it is passed to it as a property. Now, every time the store changes, the render function will be called or invoked, which accurately updates the user interface with the new state data.

Now that we have passed or processed the store to the App, we have to continue to pass it down to the child components that need it.

```
import AddColorForm from './AddColorForm'
import SortMenu from './SortMenu'
import ColorList from './ColorList'
const App = ({ store }) =>
<div className="app">
<SortMenu store={store} />
<AddColorForm store={store} />
<ColorList store={store} />
</div>
```

export the Default App

The App component is the root component. It captures the store from the props and explicitly passes it to its child components. The store is then passed on to the ColorList, AddColorForm, and SortMenu components as its property.

Now that we have already passed the store from the App, we can use it inside the child components. Remember that we can read state from the store with the help of store.getState, and we can also dispatch actions to the store with the use of store.dispatch.

From the use of AddColorForm component, we can make the store dispatch ADD_COLOR actions. When a user submits a form, we retrieve the color and title from references and utilize that information to generate and dispatch a new ADD_COLOR action:

```
import { PropTypes, Component } from 'react'import {
addColor } from '../actions'
const AddColorForm = ({store}) => {
let _title, _color
const submit = e => {
e.preventDefault()
store.dispatch( addColor(_title.value, _color.value) )
_title.value = ''
_color.value = '#000000'
_title.focus()
}
return (
<form className="add-color" onSubmit={submit}>
<input ref={input => _title = input}
type="text"
placeholder="color title..." required/>
<input ref={input => _color = input}
type="color" required/>
<button>ADD</button>
</form>
)
}
AddColorForm.propTypes = {
store: PropTypes.object
}
```

export default AddColorForm

We import the essential and vital action creator, addColor, from this component. When the user accepts the form, we utilize this action maker to send a new ADD COLOR action directly to the store.

The ColorList component may acquire the original colors and arrange them using the store's getState function. It may also immediately send RATE COLOR and REMOVE COLOR operations as they occur:

```
import { PropTypes } from 'react'
import Color from './Color'
import { rateColor, removeColor } from '../actions'
import { sortFunction } from '../lib/array-helpers'
```

```
const ColorList = ({ store }) => {
const { colors, sort } = store.getState()
const sortedColors = [...colors].
sort(sortFunction(sort))
return (
<div className="color-list">
{(colors.length === 0) ?
<p>No Colors Listed. (Add a Color)</p> :
sortedColors.map(color =>
<Color key={color.id}
{...color}
onRate={(rating) =>
store.dispatch(
rateColor(color.id, rating)
)
}
onRemove={() =>
store.dispatch(
removeColor(color.id)
)
} />
)
}
</div>
)
}
ColorList.propTypes = {
store: PropTypes.object
}
```

Export default ColorList. The store has now been passed all the way down to the component tree to the ColorList. This component interacts or communicates with the store directly. Whenever the colors are removed or rated, those actions are forwarded to the store. The store is also used to acquire the previous original colors. Those colors are duplicated and sorted, respectively, and saved as sortedColors according to the store's sort property.

sortedColors are then used to create the user interface. This technique is great if your component tree is small, like the color organizer. The disadvantage of this strategy is that we must transmit the store to the child component manually. Additionally, the ColorList, AddColorForm, and SortMenu components require this particular store. It would be difficult to reuse them in another application.

In the following sections, we will look at other ways to get the store to the components that need it. They have evolved as one of the winners in the field of Flux or Flux-like libraries. Redux is entirely based on Flux, and it was designed or created to tackle the challenge of understanding how data changes flow through the application. Redux was created by Andrew Clark and Dan abramov.

When Andrew Clark began aiding Dan with the job of finishing Redux, he was working on version 4 of Flummox, a Flux-based framework. The message on the npm page for the Flummox reads as given below:

Version 4.x should be the last and major release, but that never took place. If you want to use the recent features, then use Redux. It's very good.

Redux is surprisingly very small, with only 99 lines of code.

We have mentioned earlier that Redux is Flux-like, but it is not completely Flux. It has actions creators, action, action objects, and a store that are used to change the state. Redux clarifies the concepts of Flux a bit by eventually removing the minion, and representing App state with a single immutable object/module. Redux also introduces reducers, which are not part of the Flux pattern. Reducers are real functions that return updated states based on the current state and an action: (state, action) => newState.

State

The idea of saving the state in one place is not so crazy. In fact, we did it in the previous chapter.

We stored it in the kernel of our app. In pure React or Flux apps, storing states in as few objects as possible is recommended. In Redux, it's rule no 2.

When you came to know that you have to store state in one place, it might seem like an unnecessary requirement, especially when you have different types of data. Let's consider how this can be achieved with an App that has many different types of data.

We'll look at a social media App that has state spread out across different modules.

The application itself contains user state. All of the messages are saved in state under that. Each message contains its own state, and all of the posts are saved under the posts component.

An application structured like this may work well, but as it grows it may be hard to determine the overall state of the App. It may also become cumbersome to understand where updates have been coming from, considering that each component will mutate its own state with internal setState several calls.

What messages are expanded? What posts have been read? In order to trace these details, we must dive into the component hierarchy and track down the state inside of individual modules.

Redux clarifies the way we view state in our application by requiring us to save all state data in a single object. Everything we need to know about the App is in one place: one single source of truth. We could construct the same App with Redux by moving all of the state's data into a single location. In the social media App, we can see that we are managing the state of the current user, messages, and posts from the same object: the Redux store. This object even stores information about the message that is being edited, which messages are expanded, and which posts have been seen. This information is captured in arrays containing IDs that reference specific records. All of the messages and posts are cached in this state object, so that data is there. With Redux, we pull state management away from React entirely. Redux will manage the state.

ACTIONS

In the previous section, we introduced an important Redux rule: application state should be stored in a single immutable object. Immutable means this state object doesn't change. We will eventually update this state object by replacing it entirely. In order to do this, we will need instructions about what changes. That's what actions provide: instructions about what should change in the application state along with the necessary data to make those changes. Actions are the only way to update the state of a Redux application. Actions provide us with instructions about what should change, but we can also look at them like receipts about the history of what has changed over time. If users were to remove three colors, add four colors, and then rate five colors, they would leave a trail of information, as shown in

Usually, when we sit down to construct an object-oriented application, we start by identifying the objects, their properties, and how they work together. Our thinking, in this case, is noun-oriented. When building a Redux application, we want to shift our thinking into being verb-oriented. How will the actions affect the state data? Once you identify the actions, you can list them in a file called constants.js.

In the case of the color organizer, users will need to be able to add a color, rate a color, remove color, or sort the color list. Here we have defined a string value for each of these action types. An action is a JavaScript object that has at minimum a field for type:

```
{ type: "ADD_COLOR" }
```

The action-type is a string that defines what should happen. ADD_COLOR is the action that will add a new color to our list of colors in the application state. It is pretty easy to make typos when creating actions using strings:

```
{ type: "ADD_COOLOR" }
```

This typo would cause a bug in our application. This type of error usually does not trigger any warnings; you simply will not see the expected change of your state data.

If you make these errors, they can be tough to find. This is where constants can save you:

import C from "./constants"

```
{ type: C.ADD_COLOR }
```

This specifies the same action, but with a JavaScript constant instead of a string. A typo in a JavaScript variable will cause the browser to throw an error. Defining actions as constants also lets you tap into the benefits of IntelliSense and code completion in your IDE. When you start typing the first letter or two of a variable, the IDE will autocomplete it. Using constants is not required, but it is not a bad idea to get into the habit of incorporating them.

Action Type Naming Conventions

Action types, like ADD_COLOR or RATE_COLOR, are just strings, so technically you could call an action anything. Typically, action types are capitalized and use underscores instead of spaces. You should also aim to clearly state the action's intended purpose.

Action Payload Data

Actions are JavaScript literals that provide the instructions necessary to make a state change. Most state changes also require some data. Which record should I remove?

What new information should I provide in a new record?

We refer to this data as the action's payload. For example, when we dispatch an action like RATE_COLOR, we will need to know what color to rate and what rating to apply to that color. This information can be passed directly with the action in the same JavaScript literal.

This action tells Redux to add a new color, called Bright White, to the state. All of the information for the new color is included in the action. Actions are nice little packages that tell Redux how the state should be changed. They also include any associated data that Redux will need to make the change.

REDUCERS

Our entire state tree is stored in a single object. A potential complaint might be that it's not modular enough, possibly because you're considering modularity as describing objects. Redux achieves modularity via functions. Functions are used to update parts of the state tree. These functions are called Reducers.

Reducers are functions that take the recent state along with the action as arguments and use them to create and return a new state. Reducers are designed to update specific parts of the state tree, either leaves or branches. We can then compose reducers into one reducer that can handle updating the entire state of our App given any action. The color organizer stores all of the state data in a single tree. If we want to use Redux for this App, we can create several reducers that each target specific leaves and branches on our state tree.

This state data has two main branches: colors and sort. The sort branch is a leaf. It doesn't contain any child nodes. The color branch stores multiple colors. Each color object represents a leaf. A separate reducer will be used to handle each part of this state tree. Each reducer is simply a function, so we can stub them all at once with the code. Both the colors and color reducers will handle ADD_COLOR and RATE_COLOR. But remember, each reducer focuses on a specific part of the state tree. RATE_COLOR in the color reducer will handle the task of changing an individual color's rating value. RATE_COLOR in the colors reducer will focus on locating the color that needs to be rated in the array; ADD_COLOR in the color reducer will result in a new color object with the correct properties; ADD_COLOR in the colors reducer will return an array that has an additional color object. They are meant to work together. Each reducer focuses on what a specific action means for its branch in the state tree.

The color reducer is designed to manage leaves on the colors branch of our state tree. The colors reducer will be used to manage the entire colors branch:

```
export const colors = (state = [], action) => {
switch (action.type) {
case C.ADD_COLOR :
return [
...state,
color({}, action)
]
case C.RATE_COLOR :
return state.map(
c => color(c, action)
)
case C.REMOVE_COLOR :
return state.filter(
c => c.id !== action.id
)
default:
return state
}
}
```

The colors reducer will handle any actions for adding, rating, and removing colors.

ADD_COLOR

ADD_COLOR creates a new array by concatenating all of the values of the existing state array with a new color object. The new color is created by passing a blank state object and the action to the color reducer.

The Sort Reducer

The sort reducer is an entire function designed to manage one string variable in our state:

```
export const sort = (state = "SORTED_BY_DATE", action)
=> {
switch (action.type) {
case C.SORT_COLORS:
return action.sortBy
```

```
default :
return state
}
}
```

The sort reducer is used to change the sort state variable. It sets the sort state to the value of the action's sortBy field (if this is not state-provided, it will return SORTED_BY_DATE):

```
const state = "SORTED_BY_DATE"
const action = {
type: C.SORT_COLORS,
sortBy: "SORTED_BY_TITLE"
}
console.log( sort(state, action) ) // "SORTED_BY_TITLE"
```

To recap, state updates are handled by reducers. Reducers are pure functions that take in the state as the first argument and action as the second argument. Reducers do not cause side-effects and should treat their arguments as immutable data. In Redux, modularity is achieved through reducers. Eventually, reducers are combined into a single reducer, a function that can update the entire state tree.

In this section, we saw how reducers can be composed. We saw how the colors reducer uses the color reducer to assist in color management. In the next section, we will look at how the colors reducer can be combined with the sort reducer to update the state.

THE STORE

In Redux, the store is what holds the application's state data and handles all state updates. While the Flux design pattern allows for many stores that each focus on a the specific set of data, Redux only has one store. The store handles state updates bypassing the current state and action through a single reducer. We will create this single reducer by combining and composing all of our reducers.

If we create a store using the colors reducer, then our state object will be an array – the array of colors. The getState method of the store will return the present application state. we create a store with the color reducer, proving that you can use any reducer to create a store

In order to create a single reducer tree, we must combine the colors and sort reducers. Redux has a function for doing just that, combineReducers, which combines all of the reducers into a single reducer. These reducers are used to build your state tree. The names of the fields match the names of the reducers that are passed in.

A store can also be created with initial data. Invoking the colors reducer without state returns an empty array:

```
import { createStore, combineReducers } from 'redux'
import { colors, sort } from './reducers'
198 | Chapter 8: Redux
const store = createStore(
combineReducers({ colors, sort })
)
console.log( store.getState() )
// Console Output
//{
// colors: [],
// sort: "SORTED_BY_DATE"
//}
```

The only way to change the state of your application is by dispatching actions through the store. The store has a dispatch method that is ready to take action as an argument. When you dispatch an action through the store, the action is sent through the reducers, and the state is updated:

```
console.log(
"Length of colors array before ADD_COLOR",
store.getState().colors.length
)
// Length of colors array before ADD_COLOR 3
store.dispatch({
type: "ADD_COLOR",
id: "2222e1p5-3abl-0p523-30e4-800118yf2222",
title: "Party Pink",
color: "#F142FF",
timestamp: "Thu Mar 10 2016 01:11:12 GMT-0800 (PST)"
})
console.log(
"Length of colors array after ADD_COLOR",
store.getState().colors.length
)
// Length of colors array after ADD_COLOR 4
```

```
console.log(
"Color rating before RATE_COLOR",
store.getState().colors[3].rating
)
// Color rating before RATE_COLOR 0
store.dispatch({
type: "RATE_COLOR",
id: "2222e1p5-3ab1-0p523-30e4-800118yf2222",
rating: 5
})
console.log(
"Color rating after RATE_COLOR",
store.getState().colors[3].rating
)
// Color rating after RATE_COLOR 5
```

Here, we created a store and dispatched an action that added a new color followed by an action that changed the color's rating. The console output shows us that dispatching the actions did in fact change our state.

Originally, we had three colors in the array. We added color, and now there are four. Our new color had an original rating of zero. Dispatching an action changed it to five. The only way to change data is to dispatch actions to the store.

Subscribing to Stores

Stores allow you to subscribe to handler functions that are invoked every time the store completes dispatching an action. In the following example, we will log the count of colors in the state:

```
store.subscribe(() =>
console.log('color count:', store.getState().colors
.length)
)
store.dispatch({
type: "ADD_COLOR",
id: "2222e1p5-3ab1-0p523-30e4-800118yf2222",
title: "Party Pink",
color: "#F142FF",
timestamp: "Thu Mar 10 2016 01:11:12 GMT-0800 (PST)"
})
store.dispatch({
type: "ADD_COLOR",
id: "3315e1p5-3ab1-0p523-30e4-800118yf2412",
```

```
title: "Big Blue",
color: "#0000FF",
timestamp: "Thu Mar 10 2016 01:11:12 GMT-0800 (PST)"
})
store.dispatch({
type: "RATE_COLOR",
id: "2222e1p5-3abl-0p523-30e4-800118yf2222",
rating: 5
})
store.dispatch({
type: "REMOVE_COLOR",
id: "3315e1p5-3abl-0p523-30e4-800118yf2412"
})
// Console Output
// color count: 1
// color count: 2
// color count: 2
// color count: 1
```

Subscribing this listener to the store will log the color count to the console every time we submit an action. In the preceding example, we saw four logs: the first two for ADD_COLOR, the third for RATE_COLOR, and the fourth for REMOVE_COLOR. The subscribe method of the store returns a function that you can use later to disconnect the listener:

```
const logState = () => console.log('next state',
store.getState())
const unsubscribeLogger = store.subscribe(logState)
// Invoke when ready to unsubscribe the listener
unsubscribeLogger()
```

To recap, stores hold and manage state data in Redux applications, and the only way to change state data is by dispatching actions through the store. The store holds the application state as a single object. State mutations are managed through reducers. Stores are created by supplying a reducer along with optional data for the initial state. Also, we can subscribe listeners to our store (and unsubscribe them later), and they will be invoked every time the store finishes dispatching an action.

Both the logger and the saver are middleware functions. In Redux, middleware is defined as a higher-order function: it is a function that returns a function that returns. The last function returned is invoked each time an action is dispatched.

When this function is invoked, you have to access the action, the store, and the function for sending the request to the next middleware.

Instead of exporting the store directly, we export a function, a factory that can be used to create stores. If this factory is invoked, then it will create and return a store that incorporates logging and saving.

In the logger, before the action is dispatched, we open a new console group and log the current state and the current action. Invoking next pipes the action onto the next piece of middleware and eventually the reducers. The state at this point has been updated, so we log the changed state and end the console group.

In the saver, we invoke next with the action, which will cause the state to change. Then we save the new state in localStorage and return the result.

ADDING REDUX TO REACT

The App component is the component that holds the state. The state is passed down to child components as properties. Specifically, the colors are passed from the App component's state to the ColorList component as a property. When events happen, data is transmitted back up the component tree to the App component through callback function properties. The process of transferring data all the way down and back up the tree generates complexity that libraries like Redux are supposed to reduce. Instead of passing data up the tree through two-way function binding, we can dispatch actions directly from child components to update the application state.

In this chapter, we'll take a look at various ways to incorporate the Redux store. We will first look at how the store can be used without any additional frameworks. After that, we will explore react-redux, a framework that can be used to integrate a Redux store with React component.

Explicitly Passing the Store

The first and most obvious approach to include the store into your UI is to directly feed it down the component tree as a property. This strategy is straightforward and works well for tiny Apps with only a few hierarchical components. Let's see how we can integrate the shop into the color organizer. We will render an App component and provide it in the store in the./index.js file:

```
import React from 'react'
import ReactDOM from 'react-dom'
import App from './components/App'
```

```
import storeFactory from './store'
const store = storeFactory()
const render = () =>
ReactDOM.render(
<App store={store}/>,
document.getElementById('react-container')
)
store.subscribe(render)
render()
```

This is the ./index.js. In this code, we use the storeFactory to construct the store and render the App component into the page. The store is provided to the App as a property when it is rendered. When the store changes, the render method is called, which effectively refreshes the UI with new state data.

Now that the store has been delivered to the App, we must continue to send it down to the child components that require it:

```
import AddColorForm from './AddColorForm'
import SortMenu from './SortMenu'
import ColorList from './ColorList'
const App = ({ store }) =>
<div className="app">
<SortMenu store={store} />
<AddColorForm store={store} />
<ColorList store={store} />
</div>
```

export default App

Our base component is the App component. It reads the store from the props and explicitly sends it down to its child components. The store is supplied as a property to the SortMenu, AddColorForm, and ColorList components.

We can utilize the store that we passed from the App inside the child components now that we've passed it from the App. Remember that we can retrieve state from the store using store.getState and send actions to the store using store.dispatch.

We can utilize the store to dispatch ADD COLOR actions from the AddColorForm component. When a user submits a form, we retrieve the color and title from references and utilize that information to generate and dispatch a new ADD COLOR action:

```
import { PropTypes, Component } from 'react'
import { addColor } from '../actions'
const AddColorForm = ({store}) => {
let _title, _color
const submit = e => {
e.preventDefault()
store.dispatch( addColor(_title.value, _color.value) )
_title.value = ''
_color.value = '#000000'
```

Passing the Store via Context

We constructed a store in the previous section and sent it all the way down the component tree from the App component to the ColorList component. This technique necessitated passing the store across every component between the App and the ColorList.

Assume we have some stuff to transport from Washington, DC, to San Francisco, CA. We could utilize a train, but it would necessitate laying tracks across at least nine states in order for our shipment to reach California. This is equivalent to explicitly sending the store from the root to the leaves of the component tree. You must "lay tracks" via every component that connects the origin and destination. If taking a train is equivalent to explicitly transferring the shop through props, then passing the store implicitly via context is equivalent to taking a jet aircraft. When an aircraft travels from Washington, DC, to San Francisco, it passes over at least nine states - no rails are necessary.

Similarly, we may use context, a React feature that allows us to give variables to components without explicitly passing them down the tree as properties. These context variables are accessible to any child component.

The first step in passing the store using context in our color organizer App would be to change the App component to contain context. The App component must additionally listen to the store in order to trigger a UI update if the state changes:

```
import { PropTypes, Component } from 'react'
import SortMenu from './SortMenu'
import ColorList from './ColorList'
import AddColorForm from './AddColorForm'
import { sortFunction } from '../lib/array-helpers'
class App extends Component {
getChildContext() {
return {
```

```
store: this.props.store
}
}
componentWillMount() {
this.unsubscribe = store.subscribe(
() => this.forceUpdate()
)
}
componentWillUnmount() {
this.unsubscribe()
}
render() {
const { colors, sort } = store.getState()
const sortedColors = [...colors].
sort(sortFunction(sort))
return (
<div className="app">
<SortMenu />
<AddColorForm />
<ColorList colors={sortedColors} />
</div>
)
}
}
App.propTypes = {
store: PropTypes.object.isRequired
}
App.childContextTypes = {
store: PropTypes.object.isRequired
}
```

export default App

To begin, adding context to a component necessitates the usage of the getChildContext lifecycle method. It will return the context's defining object. In this scenario, we add the store to the context, which is accessible via props.

Then, on the component instance, give childContextTypes and construct your context object. It is analogous to adding propTypes or default-Props to a component instance. However, in order for context to function, this step must be completed.

At this moment, any children of the App component will have context access to the store. They may immediately call store.getState and store.dispatch. Finally, subscribe to the store and modify the component tree if the state of the store changes. This can be achieved with the mounting lifecycle functions. In componentWillMount, we can subscribe to the store and use this.forceUpdate to trigger the updating lifecycle, which will re-render our UI. In componentWillUnmount, we can invoke the unsubscribe function and stop listening to the store. Because the App component itself triggers the UI update, there is no need to subscribe to the store from the entry ./index.js file; we are listening to store changes from the same component that adds the store to the context, App.

Let's refactor the AddColorForm component to retrieve the store and dispatch the ADD_COLOR action directly:

```
const AddColorForm = (props, { store }) => {
let _title, _color
const submit = e => {
e.preventDefault()
store.dispatch(addColor(_title.value, _color.value))
_title.value = ''
_color.value = '#000000'
_title.focus()
}
return (
<form className="add-color" onSubmit={submit}>
<input ref={input => _title = input}
type="text"
placeholder="color title..." required/>
<input ref={input => _color = input}
type="color" required/>
<button>ADD</button>
</form>
)
}
AddColorForm.contextTypes = {
store: PropTypes.object
}
```

The context object is passed to stateless functional components as the second argument, after props. We can use object destructuring to obtain the store from this object directly in the arguments. In order to use the store, we must define contextTypes on the AddColorForm instance. This is where we tell React which context variables this component will use. This is a required step. Without it, the store cannot be retrieved from the context. Let's look at how to use context in a component class. The color component can retrieve the store and dispatch RATE_COLOR and REMOVE_COLOR actions directly:

```
import { PropTypes, Component } from 'react'
import StarRating from './StarRating'
import TimeAgo from './TimeAgo'
import FaTrash from 'react-icons/lib/fa/trash-o'
import { rateColor, removeColor } from '../actions'
class Color extends Component {
render() {
const { id, title, color, rating, timestamp } = this.props
const { store } = this.context
return (
<section className="color" style={this.style}>
<h1 ref="title">{title}</h1>
<button onClick={ () =>
store.dispatch(
removeColor(id)
)
}>
<FaTrash />
</button>
<div className="color"
style={{ backgroundColor: color }}>
</div>
<TimeAgo timestamp={timestamp} />
<div>
StarRating starsSelected={rating}
onRate={rating =>
store.dispatch(
rateColor(id, rating)
)
} />
</div>
</section>
)
}
}
Color.contextTypes = {
```

```
store: PropTypes.object
}
Color.propTypes = {
id: PropTypes.string.isRequired,
title: PropTypes.string.isRequired,
color: PropTypes.string.isRequired,
rating: PropTypes.number
}
Color.defaultProps = {
rating: 0
}
```

export default Color

ColorList is now a component class and can access context via this. context. Colors are now read directly from the store via store.getState. The same rules apply that do for stateless functional components. contextTypes must be defined on the instance. Retrieving the store from the context is a nice way to reduce your boilerplate, but this is not something that is required for every application. Dan Abramov, the creator of Redux, even suggests that these patterns do not need to be religiously followed.

Separating the containers and presentational components is frequently a smart idea, but it should not be taken as gospel. Only do this if it significantly decreases the complexity of your codebase.

SAGAS, SIDE-EFFECTS

If you want to run our Saga, we need to do the following:

- Design a Saga middleware with a list of Sagas to run/compile (so far we have only one hello_Saga).

- Connect the Saga middleware to the Redux store.

We will make the alteration to main.js:

```
// ...
import { createStore, applyMiddleware } from 'redux'
import createSagaMiddleware from 'redux-saga'
// ...
import { helloSaga } from './sagas'
const sagaMiddleware = createSagaMiddleware()
const store = createStore(
reducer,
```

```
applyMiddleware(sagaMiddleware)
)
sagaMiddleware.run(helloSaga)
const action = type => store.dispatch({type})

// rest unchanged
```

First of all, we import our Saga from the ./sagas module. Then we form a middleware with the use of the factory function to createSagaMiddleware exported through the redux-saga library.

Before running helloSaga, we should connect our middleware to the Store using the applyMiddleware. Then we would use the sagaMiddleware .run(helloSaga) to initiate our Saga.

So far, our Saga does nothing different. It just logs a message and then set back.

Making Asynchronous Calls

Now let us add something closer to the real counter demo. For illustrating asynchronous calls, we will add the other button to increase the counter one second after click.

First things first, we will provide an additional button and a callback onIncrementAsync to the user interface component.

```
const Counter = ({ value, onIncrement, onDecrement,
onIncrementAsync }) =>
<div>
<button onClick={onIncrementAsync}>
Increment after 1 second
</button>
{' '}
<button onClick={onIncrement}>
Increment
</button>
{' '}
<button onClick={onDecrement}>
Decrement
</button>
<hr />
<div>
Clicked: {value} times
</div>
</div>
```

Next, we must connect the onIncrementAsync of the module to a Store action.

We will modify this main.js module as follows:

```
function render() {
ReactDOM.render(
<Counter
value={store.getState()}
onIncrement={() => action('INCREMENT')}
onDecrement={() => action('DECREMENT')}
onIncrementAsync={() => action('INCREMENT_ASYNC')} />,
document.getElementById('root')
)
}
```

Note that unlike in redux-thunk, our component executes a simple object action.

Now, will introduce another Saga to act on the asynchronous call. Our use case is as follows:

- On each INCREMENT_ASYNC action, we need to start a task that performs following:

  - Wait for a second then increase the counter

  - Add the following codes to the sagas.js component:

```
import { put, takeEvery } from 'redux-saga/effects'
const delays = (ms) => new Promise(res =>
                       setTimeout(res, ms))
// ...

// Our worker Saga: will perform the asynchornous
                 increase task
export function* incrementAsync() {
yield delay(1000)
yield put({ type: 'INCREMENT' })
}
// Our watcher Saga: spawn a latest incrementAsync
             task on each and every INCREMENT_ASYNC
export function* watchIncrementAsync() {
yield takeEvery('INCREMENT_ASYNC', incrementAsync)
}
```

Time for the Explanations

We generate a delay function that returns a Promise that will resolve after a specified number of milliseconds. We will use this function to block the Generator.

Sagas are modified as Generator functions that yield objects to the redux-saga middleware. The yielded objects are a kind of instructions to be interpreted by the middleware. When a Promise is given to the middleware, the Saga is discarded until the Promise is completed. In the example above, the incremental sync Saga is discarded until the Promise is returned by delay resolves, which will happen after one second.

Once the Promise is sorted out, the middleware will restart the Saga, executing codes until the next yield. The following sentence is the other produced object in this example: the result of executing put (type: 'INCREMENT'), which informs the middleware to dispatch an INCREMENT action.put is an example of what we call an Effect. Effects are plain JavaScript objects which have instructions to be fulfilled by the middleware. When a middleware recovers an Effect yielded by the Saga, the Saga is paused until the Effect is fulfilled.

So as to summarize, the incremental sync Saga sleeps for 1(one) second via the call to delay(1000), then dispatches an INCREMENT call.

Next, we design another Saga watchIncrementAsync. We use takeEvery, a helper or composite function provided by redux-saga, to listen for dispatched INCREMENT_ASYNC actions or calls and run incrementAsync each time.

Now there are two Sagas, and we require to execute them both at once. To do that, we will add a rootSaga that is responsible for starting our other Sagas. In the file sagas.js, refactor the file as follows:

```
import { put, takeEvery, all }from 'redux-saga/
        effects'
const delays = (ms) => new Promise(res =>
                        setTimeout(res, ms))
function* helloSaga() {
console.log('Hello Saga!')
}
function* incrementAsync() {
yield delay(1000)
yield put ({ type: 'INCREMENT' })
}
```

```
function* watchIncrement_Async() {
yield take_Every('INCREMENT-ASYNC', incrementAsync)
}

// Notice how do we now only export the rootSaga////
one entry point to start all Sagas at once
export default function* rootSaga() {
yield all([
helloSaga(),
watchIncrementAsync()
])
}
```

This Saga yields an array with the consequence of calling our two sagas, helloSaga and watchIncrementAsync. This means that the two resulting Generators will be executed in parallel. Now we only have to call on sagaMiddleware.run on the root Saga in main.js.

```
// ...
import rootSaga from './sagas'
const sagaMiddleware = createSagaMiddleware()
const store = ...
sagaMiddleware.run(rootSaga)

// ...
```

Redux Saga is a middleware library that allows a Redux store to interact with the resources outside of itself asynchronously. This includes making HTTP(HyperText Mat requests to external services, accessing browser storage, and executing I/O actions. These actions are also known as side-effects. Redux Saga helps to manage these side-effects in a way that is easier to manage.

A redux store intrinsically knows how to dispatch actions and update its state using its root reducer. Actions constitute an event describing something happening in your App and an intention to modify your app's state. A reducer accumulates value from or stemming from dispatched actions and accumulates these values into the newly updated state of your application.

Reducers have been defining in as pure functions, as it is compulsory to let useful attributes of Redux such as time travel (re-playing past calls). Actions are objects or arguments passed on into the reducer and are naturally positive. Thus, we have a problem; there is nowhere in your Redux application to place your side-effects.

A Redux middleware is associated between an action and a reducer. This allows actions to contain something else other than the plain object, as long as the middleware intercepts this, performs its functionality, and returns a plain object to pass along toward the reducer.

Redux Thunk, a popular Redux-Saga option, allows functions to enter the Redux store dispatch, which checks to see if it is a function or an action object or module, starting the component in the former scenario and directly passing along with the action objects to the reducer in the latter case, and these functions can then perform whatever composite asynchronous logic they want and produce a plain action or call object to be passed into the reducer.

Redux Sagas are somewhat different in that a separate set of instructions are defined in your Redux app, which is captured exclusively by watcher functions (as part of your saga). The saga will implement the corresponding logic and dispatch a resultant call to your App's reducer upon capturing the calls. The saga effectively operates as a second thread to your App, listening for particular actions from your main application to do sophisticated asynchronous activities and changing the state of your App once they are completed.

While I would not say Redux Saga is inherently better than any of the alternatives available, it has some benefits that might make you want to consider its use.

Redux Saga offers a place completely de-coupled from your action makers for you to handle your App's side-effects. Some people may feel that this makes your App's data flow harder to follow (which I would agree with), but I think that this de-coupling makes organizing your codebase and extending functionality simpler down the road.

For example, in a situation where you might require to support a workflow that needs multiple HTTP requests to different services in a particular order, Redux-Saga permits you to compose granular sagas into a single one and represents this new high-level function with a separate call. Your application can still access/pass each individual HTTP resource in another workflow, but for this specific one, your React component can manually call this high-level action to load whatever it requires from a single place. As far as your component or module is concerned, your asynchronous logic to load multiple resources in a particular order is an abstracted way.

Redux Saga also offers a collection of composite functions that are used to spawn your works when some specific calls are dispatched. These can be used to help in managing when and how your tasks are implemented.

Let us take an example that the most commonly used helper function is takeEvery(). This instructs the middleware to spawn a new task for every action dispatched to your store similar to a given pattern. This provides a behavior identical to Redux Thunk and is as simple as it gets: "Application reminds you to fetch something, go and fetch it."

Now think that you had two functionally independent components or modules that needed to retrieve the most updated data from the place. Previously they existed on two pages and could be visited on it at any time. It would make sense for both components or modules to try to retrieve a new copy of the resource whenever it is rendered. Now imagine that your features have changed, and now the two components need to be on the same page, and now you have a situation where two different components are redundantly spawning the same task.

You could mention one of the components to no longer try to retrieve a new copy and rely on the other to design the necessary action or calls to retrieve this resource and populate the App store. Or you could add some logic concept to ensure that your component does not try to form a new action to retrieve this resource if this resource is already being loaded or mounted. But this could also be solved using the other Redux-Saga helper function: take(). This function instructs the middleware to spawn a new task for an action dispatched matching a given pattern but will effectively ignore any new actions until the spawned task has been completed.

With this, your two independent components or modules can coexist without changing any component-specific logic! As far as your component is concerned, it asks your saga to retrieve resources on its behalf and retrieve them from the resultant updated states. Your saga gets to decide how to do it and wants to consider two different requests from different components. It is packed full of useful examples if you'd like to get into the low-level details.

Redux Saga is one of several tools to help you organize your App's side-effects. It is heavy and has a learning curve but contains a lot of functionality that will help keep your codebase neat and modular to make the code testable.

We need to test our incrementAsync Saga to make sure it performs the desired task.

Create Another File Sagas.spec.js

```
import test from 'tape'
import { incrementAsync } from './sagas'
test('incrementAsync Saga test', (assert) => {
const generator = incrementAsync()
// now what ?
})
```

When incrementAsync is called, it produces an iterator object, and the iterator's next method returns an object of the following structure.

```
generator.next() // => { done: boolean, value: any }
```

The value field keeps the yielded expression, i.e., the result of the expressions after the yield. The done field identifies if the generator has terminated/halts or if there are still have 'yield' expressions.

In the case of incremental sync, the generator creates two values consecutively:

```
yield delay(1000)
yield put({type: 'INCREMENT'})
```

So, if we call on the next method/function of the generator three times consecutively, we get the results as follows:

```
generator.next() // => { done: false, value: <result
                         of calling delay(1000)> }
generator.next() // => { done: false, value: <result
                   of calling put({type: 'INCREMENT'})> }
generator.next() // => { done: true, value: un_
                         defined }
```

The first two invocations return the results of the yield expressions. On the third citation, since there is no more yield, the done field is set to true value. And since the incrementAsync Generator doesn't return anything (no return statement), the value field is set to undefined or void.

So now in order to test the functionality inside the incrementAsync, we will have to repeat over the returned Generator and test the values yielded/generated by the generator.

```
import test from 'tape'
import { incrementAsync } from './sagas'
test('incrementAsync Saga test', (assert) => {
const generation = incrementAsync()
assert.deepEqual(
generator.next(),
{ done: false, value: ??? },
'incrementAsync should return a Promise that will sort
            out after one second'
)
})
```

The issue is how do we test the returns value of the delay? We cannot do a simple test of equality on Promises and if delay returned a normal value, things would have been simpler to test.

Well, redux-saga provides the way to make the above statement possible. Despite calling delay(1000) directly inside incrementAsync, we will call it indirectly and export it to make a subsequent deep matching feasible:

```
import { put, take_Every, all, call } from 'redux-
saga/effects'
export const delays = (ms) => new Promise(res =>
                        setTimeout(res, ms))
// ...
export function* incrementAsync() {
// use the call Effect
yield call(delay, 1000)
yield put({ type: 'INCREMENT' })
}
```

In place of doing yield delay(1000), we're now doing yield call(delay, 1000). What is the difference?

In case 1, the yield expression delay(1000) is assessed before it gets passed to the call of next (the caller could be the middleware when running our codes. It could also be our test code that runs or compiles the Generator function and repeats over the returned Generator). So what the caller get is a Promise, as in the above test code.

In case 2, the yield expression call(delay, 1000) is required to the caller of the next call just like put, and returns an Effect that instructs the middleware to call a given function with the given argument sets. In fact, neither the put nor call performs any dispatch or asynchronous call by itself, they return plain JavaScript objects or functions.

```
put({type: 'INCREMENT'}) // => { PUT: {type:
                                     'INCREMENT'} }
call(delay, 1000) // => { CALL: {fn: delays, args:
                                     [1000] }}
```

What happens is that the middleware checks the type of each yielded Effect, then decides how to attain that Effect. It will convey an action to the Store if the Effect type is a PUT. It will call the given function if the Effect is a CALL.

This separation between Effect formation and Effect execution makes it possible to test our Generator in a surprisingly easy way:

```
import test from 'tape'
import { put, call } from 'redux-saga/effects'
import { incrementAsync, delay } from './sagas'
test('incrementAsync Saga test', (assert) => {
const gen = incrementAsync()
assert.deepEqual(
gen.next().value,
call(delay, 1000),
'incrementAsync Saga must call delay(1000)'
)
assert.deepEqual(
gen.next().value,
put({type: 'INCREMENT'}),
'incrementAsync Saga must dispatch an INCREMENT action'
)
assert.deepEqual(
gen.next(),
{ done: true, value: undefined },
'incrementAsync Saga must be done'
)
assert.end()
})
```

CHAPTER 10

Forms

IN THIS CHAPTER

➢ Forms

➢ Form validation

Forms are the first and the most basic of HTML. We use the HyperText Markup Language form element to create the JavaScript form. Form name tags are used to define the name of the form used. The name of the form here is "Login-form." This name will be referenced in the JS form used in the program.

The action tag is used to define the action, and the browser will be used to tackle the form when it is going to be submitted. Here, we have taken no action against anyone.

When the form is to be sent to the server, the mechanism to take action might be either post or get. Both techniques have their own set of characteristics and directions.

The input type tag states the type of inputs we want to generate in our form. Here, we have declared the input type as "text," which means that we will input values as text in the textbox.

Next, we have taken the input type as "password" and the input values will be password.

Moving ahead, we have taken input type as "button," where on clicking, we get the value of the form and get displayed.

DOI: 10.1201/9781003309369-10

Other than action and approaches, there are subsequent useful approaches also which are provided by the HTML form element.

- **submit** (): The technique is used to submit the form.

- **reset** (): The technique is used to reset the form values.

REFERENCING FORMS

Now, we have formed the form element using HTML, but we are also required to make its connectivity to JS. For this, we use the getElement-ById () process that references the HTML form element to the JavaScript codes.

The syntax of using the getElementById() method or techniques is as follows:

let form = document.getElementById('Hello');Using the Id, we can make the orientation.

Submitting the Form

Next, we want to submit the form by submitting its value reference, for which we use the onSubmit() process. Mostly, to submit, we use a submit button that submits the value typed in the form.

The following is the syntax for the submit() method:

```
<input type="submit" value="Subscribe">
```

When we submit the form, an action is taken right before the request is submitted to the server, and it allows us to add an event auditor that allows us to apply multiple authentications on the form. Finally, the form gets ready with a blend of HTML and JavaScript codes.

Let us collect and use all these to form a Login form and SignUp form and use both.

Login Form

```
html>
<head>
<title> Login-Form</title>
</head>
<body>
<h3> LOGIN HERE </h3>
```

```
<formform ="Login_form" onsubmit="submit_form()">
<h4> USERNAME</h4>
<input type="text" placeholder="Enter your e-mail id"/>
<h4> PASSWORD</h4>
<input type="password" placeholder="Enter the
password"/></br></br>
<input type="submit" value="Login"/>
<input type="button" value="Sign_Up" onClick="create()"/>
</form>
<script type="text/javascript">
function submit_form(){
alert("Login Successfully");
}
function create(){
window.location="signup.html";
}
</script>
</body>
</html>
```

Output of the above code:

SignUp Form

```
<html>
<head>
<title> Sign_Up Page</title>
</head>
<body align="center" >
<h1> CREATE YOUR ACCOUNT IN A FEW STEPS</h1>
<table cellspacing="2" align="center" cellpadding="8"
                                    border="0">
<tr><td> Name</td>
<td><input type="text" placeholder="Enter your full
                    name" id="n1"></td></tr>
<tr><td>Email </td>
<td><input type="text" placeholder="Enter your e-mail
                    id" id="e1"></td></tr>
<tr><td> Set Password</td>
<td><input type="password" placeholder="Set the
                password" id="p1"></td></tr>
<tr><td>Confirm Password</td>
<td><input type="password" placeholder="Confirm your
                password" id="p2"></td></tr>
```

```
<tr><td>
<input type="submit" value="Create"
                    onClick="create_account()"/>
</table>
<script type="text/javascript">
function create_account(){
var n=document.getElementById("n1").value;
var e=document.getElementById("e1").value;
var p=document.getElementById("p1").value;
var cp=document.getElementById("p2").value;
//Codes for password confirmation
var letters = /^[A-Za-z]+$/;
var email_val = /^([a-zA-Z0-9_\.\-])+\@(([a-zA-Z0-9
                \-])+\.)+([a-zA-Z0-9]{2,4})+$/;
//other confirmations required codes
if(n==''||e==''||p==''||cp==''){
alert("Enter each details correctly");
}
else if(!letters.test(n))
{
alert('Name i must contain alphabets only');
}
else if (!email_val.test(e))
{
alert('Invalid e-mail format please enter valid e-mail
id');
}
else if(p!=cp)
{
alert("Passwords not matching");
}
else if(document.getElementById("p1").value.length >
12)
{
alert("Password maximum length is 12");
}
else if(document.getElementById("p1").value.length <
6)
{
alert("Password minimum length is 6");
}
else{
```

```
alert("Your account has been formed successfully... ");
}
}
</script>
</body>
</html>
```

EVENT BUBBLING AND CAPTURING IN JAVASCRIPT

In JavaScript, dissemination of measures is done, which is known as "Event Flow." The arrangement or sequence in which the event is received by the specific web page is referred to as event flow. Thus, in JS, the event flow process is dependent on three factors:

1. Event capturing

2. Event target

3. Event bubbling

The notion of event bubbling is utilized while constructing a web page or a website using JS, where event managers are summoned when one element is nested into the other element and is part of the same occurrence. This approach or procedure is called as event bubbling, and it is utilized while executing event flow for a web page. We can understand event bubbling as a classification of calling the event handlers when one element is nested into the other element, and both the elements have registered listeners for the same event. So, commencement from the deepest component to its parents covering all its ancestors on the way to top to lowest, call is performed.

Example of Event Bubbling

Let us look at the example to appreciate the working concept of event bubbling:

```
<!DOCTYPE html>
<html>
<head>
<meta charset="utf-8">
<meta name="viewport" content="width=device-width">
<title>Event Bubbling</title>
```

```
</head>
<body>
<div id="p1">
<button id="c1">I am the child button</button>
</div>
<script>
var parent = document.querySelector('#p1');
parent.addEventListener('click', function(){
console.log("Parent has invoked");
});
var child = document.querySelector('#c1');
child.addEventListener('click', function(){
console.log("Child has invoked");
});
</script>
</body>
</html>
```

The Output of the above Code

Explanation of the above Code

The above code is an HTML and JavaScript-based code.

We have used the div tag with div id = p1 and inside div, we have nested a button with button id = c1.

Now, within the JavaScript segment, we have allocated the HTML elements (p1 and c1) using the querySelector () function to the adjustable parent and the child.

After that, we have formed and included an event which is the click incident to both the div element and child button. Also are formed two functions that will help us to know the sequence of the execution of the parent and the child. It means that if the child event is appealed first, "child has invoked" will be printed, then "parent is invoked" will get printed on the console window.

Thus, when the button is clicked, it will first print "child has invoked," which means that the function within the child event handler performs first. Then it goes to the invocation of the div parent function.

The arrangement has taken place due to the perception of the event bubbling. Thus, in this way event bubbling takes place.

Stopping Bubbling

Beginning from the target and moving ahead toward the top of the bubbling, i.e., starting from the child to its paternal, it moves straight upward. A handler can also decide to stop the bubbling when the event has been treated entirely. In JavaScript, we use the event.stopPropagation () method.

Example:

```
<!DOCTYPE html>
<html>
<head>
<meta charset="utf-8">
<meta name="viewport" content="width=device-width">
<title>Event Bubbling</title>
</head>
<body>
<div id="p1">
<button id="c1" onclick="event.stopPropagation()">I
                              am the child</button>
</div>
<script>
var parent = document.querySelector('#p1');
parent.addEventListener('click', function(){
console.log("Parent is invoked");
});
var child = document.querySelector('#c1');
child.addEventListener('click', function(){
console.log("Child is invoked");
});
</script>
</body>
</html>
```

In order to invoke the bubbling and also prevent the handlers from running on the current component, we can use event.stopImmediatePropagation () process. It is another way that stops the bubbling and implementation of all the other handlers. This implies that if a component contains more than one event handler on a single event, all event handlers that are bubbling will be stopped using this event.stopImmediatePropagation() method.

Event Capturing

Netscape Browser was the first browser to introduce the method of event capturing. Event capturing is contradictory to event bubbling; in event capturing, an event moves from the outer-most element to the target, whereas in the case of event bubbling, the event movement begins from the target to the outer-most element in the file, and event capturing is achieved before event bubbling but capturing is used very rarely for the reason that event bubbling is sufficient to handle the event flow.

Example of Event Capturing

Let us consider an example code to understand the working of event capturing.

```
<!DOCTYPE html>
<html>
<head>
<meta charset="utf-8">
<meta name="viewport" content="width=device-width">
<title>Event Capturing</title>
</head>
<body>
<div id="p1">
<button id="c1">I am Child</button>
</div>
<script>
var parent = document.querySelector('#p1');
var child = document.querySelector('#c1');
parent.addEventListener('click', function(){
console.log("Parent is invoked");
},true);
child.addEventListener('click', function(){
console.log("Child is invoked");
});
</script>
</body>
</html>
```

Explanation of Code

The above-described codes are based on HTML and JS.

In the HTML portion, we have formed a div id holding id = p1. Inside the div, we have nested and formed a button with id = c1.

Moving on to the JS scripts, we've used the querySelector () procedure to assign the HTML element, i.e., the p1 id, to variable parent, and we've done the same with the c1 id, which we've assigned to a changeable child.

Then we have used the click event and attached it to both the p1 div and c1 buttons. It also has a function for printing the suitable message on the console. It indicates that if the child event handler is executed first, the console screen will display the "Child is invoked" message, and if the parent event handler is invoked first, the console screen will display the "Parent is invoked" message.

Next, we have added the third argument of addEventListner () to true in order to allow event capturing in the parent div.

When we click on this button, it first performs the function attached to the parent div.

Later, the onclick () function of the button runs or executes, and this is due to event capturing, and owing to event capturing, the event of the parent element is completed first, followed by the event of the target element.

Redux has emerged as one of the unambiguous victors in the Flux or Flux-like libraries sector. Redux is built on Flux and was developed to address the issues of evaluating how data changes move through your project. Dan Abramov and Andrew Clark created and designed Redux. Both have been hired by Facebook to work on the React team since developing Redux. When Andrew Clark began aiding Dan with the effort of finalizing Redux, he was working on version 4 of Flummox, the other Flux-based library. The message on the npm pages for Flummox reads: Eventually 4.x should be the last major issue but it never happened. If you want the latest attributes, then use Redux instead. It is really great.

Redux is surprisingly small and precise, with only 99 lines of code.

We have stated that Redux is Flux-like, but it is not precisely Flux. It has actions, action makers, a store, and action objects that are used to alter the state. Redux simplifies the concepts or methods of Flux a bit by eliminating the dispatcher and representing App states with a single unchallengeable object. Redux also introduces the reducers, which are not a part of Flux patterns. Reducers are the pure functions that return a new state based on the existing states and an action: (state, action) => newState.

State

The concept of storing state in a single location is not that far-fetched. We really accomplished that in the previous chapter. We saved it in the

App's root directory. In pure the React or Flux apps, storing state in as few objects as possible is recommended. In Redux, it is a rule.2 When you hear that you have to save states in one place, it might seem like an unreasonable requirement, specifically when you have dissimilar types of data. Let us consider how this can be achieved with an App with many different types of data, and we will look at a social media App with states spread out across diverse components. The App itself has user states. All of the messages are stored in state under that, each message has its own states, and all of the posts are saved under the posts component.

An application structured like this may work well, but as it raises it may be hard to determine the overall state of the App. It may also become bulky to understand where updates are coming from, seeing that each component will change its own state with interior setState calls. What messages are expanded? What posts have been read? To figure out these facts, we must dive into the component tree and track down the state inside of discrete components. The idea of keeping state in a single location isn't so far-fetched. We stored it in the root directory of the program. We could construct the same App with Redux by moving all of the state data into a single position

ACTIONS

The previous section introduced a significant Redux rule: App state should be stored in a single unchallengeable object. Immutable means this state object does not change. We will finally update this state object by replacing it completely. In order to do this, we will require commands about what changes. Actions provide instructions about what should change in the App state and the necessary data to make those alters. Actions are the only way to update the state of a Redux App. Actions provide us with commands about what should alter, but we can also look at them like receipts about the history of what has altered over time. If users were to eliminate three colors, add four colors, and then rate five colors, they would leave a trail of info usually; when we sit down to construct an object-oriented App, we start by recognizing the objects, their properties, and how they work when organized. Our thinking, in this case, is noun-oriented. When building a Redux App, we want to shift our thinking into being verb-oriented. How will the actions affect the data of the state? Once you classify the actions, you can list them in a file called constants.js.

Action Payload Data

Actions are JavaScript literals that provide the commands essential to make a state change. Most state changes also need some data. Which record should I remove? What new info should I afford in a new record? We refer to this data as the action's payload. For example, when we dispatch an action like RATE_COLOR, we will want to know what color to rate and what rating to apply to that color. This info can be passed right with the action in the same Java Script literal (see the following Example).

Example: RATE_COLOR action

```
{
type: "RATE_COLOR",
id: "a5685c39-6bdc-4727-9188-6c9a00bf7f95"
Redux Docs, "Reducers".

}
```

This action states Redux to add a new color called Bright White to the states. All of the info for the new color is involved in the action. Actions are nice little packages that tell Redux how the state should alter. They also include any related data that Redux will need to modify. In Reducers, our entire state tree is saved in a single object. A potential complaint might be that it is not modular enough, possibly because you consider modularity as relating objects. Redux attains modularity via functions. Functions are used to update parts of the state tree. These functions are termed reducers.

Reducers are functions that take the existing state along with action as arguments and use them to form and return a new state. Reducers are intended to update precise parts of the state tree, either leaves or branches, and we can then compose reducers into one reducer that can handle updating the entire state of our application given any action. The color coordinator stores all of the state data in a single tree, and if we want to use Redux for this application, we can form several reducers that each target precise leaves and branches on our state's tree.

The HTML DOM permits JavaScript to alter the style of HTML elements.

Changing HTML Style

To modify or alter the style of an HTML element, use this syntax:

Document.getElementById(id).style.property = new style

The subsequent example changes the style of a <p> element:

Example:

```
<html>
<body>
<p id="p2">Hello World!</p>
<script>
Document.getElementById("p2").style.color = "blue";
</script>
</body>
</html>
```

Using Events

The HTML DOM lets you execute codes when an event occurs.

Events are created by the browser when "things happen" to HTML elements:

- An element is clicked on

- The page has loaded

- Input fields are altered

In this example, changes in the style of the HTML element with id="id1", when the user clicks a button:

Example:

```
<!DOCTYPE html>
<html>
<body>
<h1 id="id1">My_Heading 1</h1>
<button type="button"
Onclick="document.getElementById('id1').style.color =
'red'">
Click_Me!</button>
</body>
</html>
```

JavaScript(JS) Form Validation

HTML form validation can be done by the JavaScript(JS).

If a form field (fname) is blank, this function alerts a message, and returns false value to prevent the form from being submitted:

JS Example:
```
Function validateForm() {
Let x = document.forms["myForm"]["fname"].value;
If (x == "") {
Alert("Name must be filled out");
Return false;
}
}
```

When the form is submitted, the following function can be called:

HTML Form Example:
```
<form name="myForm" action="/action_page.php"
onsubmit="return validateForm()" method="post">
Name: <input type="text" name="fname">
<input type= "submit" value="Submit">
</form>
```

JavaScript can confirm numeric input.
JavaScript is often used to authorize numeric input:
Please input the number between 1 and 10
Submit

Automatic HTML Form Authentication
HTML form authentication can be performed automatically by the browser.

If a form field (fname) is blank, the required features prevents this form from being submitted:

HTML Form Example:

```
<form action="/action_page.php" method="post">
<input type="text" name="fname" required>
<input type="submit" value="Submit">
</form>
```

Automatic HTML form authentication does not work in Internet Explorer 9 or earlier.

DATA VALIDATION

Data validation is the process of confirming that user input is clean, correct, and useful.

Typical validation tasks are:

- Has the user filled in all mandatory fields?

- Has the user filled a valid date?

- Has the user filled text in a numeric field?

Most often, data authentication aims to ensure correct user input.

Validation can be defined by many different approaches and deployed in several ways.

A web server executes server-side validation after the input has been sent to the server.

A web browser executes client-side validation before the input is sent to a web server.

HTML CONSTRAINT VALIDATION

HTML5 introduced a new HTML validation method called constraint validation.

HTML constraint validation is based on:

- Constraint validation HTML Input Features

- Constraint validation CSS Pseudo Selectors

- Constraint validation DOM Properties and Approaches

- Constraint Validation HTML Input Attributes

ATTRIBUTE DESCRIPTION

- Disabled specifies that the input element should be disabled.

- Max specifies the extreme value of an input element.

- Min specifies the lowest value of an input element.

- Pattern specifies the value patterns of an input element.

- Required specifies that the input field needs an element.

- Type specifies the type of an input element.

For a full list, go to HTML Input Attributes.

CONSTRAINT VALIDATION CSS PSEUDO SELECTORS

- Selector explanation

  - :disabled Selects input elements with the "disabled" feature detailed

  - :invalid Selects input elements with invalid values

  - :optional Selects input elements with no "required" feature specified

  - :required Selects input elements with the "required" feature specified

  - :valid Selects input elements with valid v

- JavaScript HTML DOM animation

LEARN TO CREATE HTML ANIMATIONS USING JAVASCRIPT
A Basic Web Page

To determine how to make HTML animations with JavaScript, we will use a simple web page:

Example:

```
<!DOCTYPE html>
<html>
<body>
<h1>My First JavaScript Animation Tutorial</h1>
<div id="animation">My animation will go from here</
div>
</body>
</html>
```

CREATE AN ANIMATION CONTAINER

All animations should be the relative to a container element.

Example:

```
<div id ="container">
<div id ="animate">My animation will go from here</div>
</div>
```

STYLE THE ELEMENTS

The container element should be formed with style = "position: relative."

The animation element should be formed with style = "position: absolute."

Example:

```
#container {
Width: 400px;
Height: 400px;
Position: relative;
Background: yellow;
}
#animate {
Width: 50px;
Height: 50px;
Position: absolute;
Background: red;
}
```

ANIMATION CODE

JavaScript animations are done by steady programming modification in an element's style.

A timer calls the change. When the timer interval is minor, the animation looks continuous.

The basic codes is:

Example:

```
Id = setInterval(frame, 5);
Function frame() {
If (/* test for finished */) {
clearInterval(id);
} else {
/* codes to modify the element style */
}
}
```

Create the Full Animation Using JavaScript JS

Example:

```
Function myMove() {
Let id = null;
Const elem = document.getElementById("animate");
```

```
Let pos = 0;
clearInterval(id);
id = setInterval(frame, 5);
function frame() {
if (pos == 350) {
clearInterval(id);
} else {
Pos++;
Elem.style.top = pos + 'px';
Elem.style.left = pos + 'px';
}
}
}
```

JavaScript can be accomplished when an event occurs, like when a user clicks on an HTML element.

To accomplish code when a user clicks on an element, add JavaScript codes to an HTML event feature:

Onclick=JavaScript

Examples of HTML events:

- When a user clicks the mouse
- When a web page has loaded
- When an image has been loaded
- When the mouse moves over an element
- When an input field is changed
- When an HTML form is submitted
- When a user strokes a key

In the following example, the content of the <h1> element is changed when a user clicks on it:

  Example:

```
<!DOCTYPE html>
<html>
<body>
```

```
<h1 onclick="this.innerHTML = 'Ooops!'">Click on the
                                     text!</h1>
</body>
</html>
```

In the below example, a function is called from the event handler:
Example:

```
<!DOCTYPE html>
<html>
<body>
<h1 onclick="changeText(this)">Click on the text!</h1>
<script>
Function changeText(id) {
Id.innerHTML = "Ooops!";
}
</script>
</body>
</html>
```

FORM VALIDATION

Form validation in React allows an error or bug message to be displayed if the user has not properly filled out the form with the expected type of input.

There are numerous ways to authorize forms in React; however, this shot will focus on generating a validator function with validation rules

The codes below assume that the user is familiar with the technique and elements required to make a React form. The form validation rules are used in the handleChange function, which processes user input.

A React functional component is a simple JavaScript function that accepts props and returns a React element.

After the introduction of React Hooks, writing functional components has become the standard way of writing React components in modern Apps.

STYLE THE ELEMENTS

- The container element should be designed with style = "position: relative."

- The animation element should be designed with style = "position: absolute."

Example:

```
#container {
width: 400px;
height: 400px;
position: relative;
background: yellow;
}
#animate {
width: 50px;
height: 50px;
position: absolute;
background: red;
}
```

ANIMATION CODE

JavaScript animations are done by programming steady variations in an element's style. The changes are called by the timer. When the timer interval is small, the animation looks continuous.

The basic codes is:

```
id = setInterval(frame, 5);

function frame() {
if (/* test for finished */) {
clearInterval(id);
} else {
/* codes to modify the element style */
}
}
```

Design the Full Animation Using JavaScript

Example:

```
function myMove() {
let id = null;
const elem = document.getElementById("animate");
let pos = 0;
clearInterval(id);
id = setInterval(frame, 5);
function frame() {
if (pos == 350) {
```

```
clearInterval(id);
} else {
pos++;
elem.style.top = pos + 'px';
elem.style.left = pos + 'px';
}
}
}
```

The addEventListener() process

Example:

Add the event listener that fires when a user clicks on the button:

```
document.getElementById("myBtn").addEventListener(
                    "click", displayDate);
```

- The addEventListener() process attaches an event handler to the definite element.

- The addEventListener() process assigns an event handler to an element without overwriting present event handlers.

- You may add as many event handlers as you like to a single element.

- You can add as many event handlers of the same type to one element, i.e. two "click" events.

- You can also add event listeners to any DOM object, not only HTML elements. i.e., the window object.

- The addEventListener() method makes it easier to regulate how the event reacts to the bubbling.

- When using the addEventListener() method or technique, the JavaScript is detached from the HTML markup, for better readability, and lets you add the event listeners even when you don't control the HTML markup.

- You can easily remove the event listener by using the removeEventListener() method or techniques.

Syntax

```
element.addEventListener(event, function, useCapture);
```

The first argument is the event type (like "click" or "mousedown" or any other HTML DOM Event.)

The second parameter is the function we need to call when the event happens.

The third parameter is a boolean value requiring whether to use event bubbling or event capturing. This parameter is optional.

Note that you do not use the "on" prefix for the event; use "click" in its place of "onclick."

Add the Event Handler to an Element

Example:

Alert "Hello_World!" when the user clicks on an element.

```
element.addEventListener("click", function(){
                    alert("Hello_World!"); });
```

You can also refer to external "named" fun:

Example:

Alert "Hello_World!" when the user clicks on an element.

DOM NODES

According to the W3C HTML DOM standards, everything in an HTML document is the node:

- The entire document is the document node

- Every HTML element is the element node

- The text inside HTML elements are the text nodes

- Every HTML feature is an attribute node (deprecated)

- All comments are comment nodes

DOM HTML TREE

With the HTML DOM, all the nodes in the node hierarchy can be retrieved by JavaScript JS.

New nodes can be designed, and all nodes can be altered or deleted.

NODE RELATIONSHIPS

Nodes in the node tree are connected in a hierarchical manner.

The terms parent, child, and sibling node are used to define the relationships.

In the node tree, the top node has termed the root(or root node).

Every node has precisely one parent, except the root (which has no parent).

A node can have numerous children.

Siblings (brothers or sisters) are nodes with the same parent.

```
<html>
<head>
<title>DOM_Tutorial</title>
</head>
<body>
<h1>DOM Lesson 1</h1>
<p>Hello_world!</p>
</body>
</html>
```

Node Tree

From the above HTML you can read:

```
<html> is the root node
<html> has no parents node
<html> is the parent node of the <head> and <body>
<head> is the first child node of <html>
<body> is the last child node of <html>
```

and:

```
<head> has one child node: <title>
<title> has one child node (a text node): "DOM Tutorials"
<body> has two children: <h1> and <p>
<h1> has one child: "DOM Lesson 1"
<p> has one child: "Hello_world!"
<h1> and <p> are siblings
```

NAVIGATING BETWEEN NODES

You can use the subsequent node properties to navigate among nodes with JavaScript JS:

```
parentNode
childNodes[nodenumber]
firstChild
```

```
lastChild
nextSibling
previousSibling
```

Child Nodes and Node Values

A common error in the DOM processing is to expect an element node to hold text.

Example:

```
<title id="demo">DOM_Tutorial</title>
```

The element node <title> (in the above example) does not hold text.
It contains the text node with the value "DOM_Tutorial."

The value of the text nodes can be retrieved by the node's innerHTML property:

```
myTitle = document.getElementById("demo").innerHTML;
```

Retrieving the innerHTML property is the same as accessing the node-Value of the first child:

```
myTitle = document.getElementById("demo").firstChi
                              ld.nodeValue;
```

Retrieving the first child can also be done are this:

```
myTitle = document.getElementById("demo").childNod
es[0].nodeValue;
```

All the (3) subsequent examples retrieve the text of an <h1> element and copies it into a <p> element:

Example:

```
<html>
<body>
<h1 id="id01">My First_Page</h1>
<p id="id02"></p>
<script>
document.getElementById("id02").innerHTML = document.g
etElementById("id01").innerHTML;
</script>
</body>
</html>
```

Example:

```
<html>
<body>
<h1 id="id01">My First_Page</h1>
<p id="id02"></p>
<script>

document.getElementById("id02").innerHTML = document.g
etElementById("id01").firstChild.nodeValue;

</script>
</body>
</html>
```

Example:

```
<html>
<body>
<h1 id="id01">My First_Page</h1>
<p id="id02">Hello World !</p>
<script>

document.getElementById("id02").innerHTML = document.g
etElementById("id01").childNodes[0].nodeValue;

</script>
</body>
</html>
```

InnerHTML

In this section, we use the inner HTML property to retrieve the content of an HTML element.

However, learning the other approaches above is useful for understanding the tree (hierarchy) structure and the navigation of the DOM.

DOM ROOT NODES

There are two special properties that let access to the full document:

1. **document.body**: The body of a document

2. **document.documentElement**: The full document

Example:

```
<html>
<body>
<h2>JavaScript JS HTMLDOM</h2>
<p>Displaying document.body</p>
<p id="demo"></p>
<script>

document.getElementById("demo").innerHTML = document
.body.innerHTML;

</script>
</body>
</html>
```

Example:

```
<html>
<body>
<h2>JavaScript JS HTMLDOM</h2>
<p>Displaying document.documentElement</p>
<p id="demo"></p>
<script>
document.getElementById("demo").innerHTML = document.
documentElement.innerHTML;
</script>
</body>
</html>
```

The nodeName Property

- The nodeName property specify the name of a node.

- nodeName is read-only.

- nodeName of an element node is the similar as the tag name.

- nodeName of a feature node is the features name.

- nodeName of the text node is always #text.

- nodeName of the document node always the #document.

Example:

```
<h1 id="id01">My First_Page</h1>
<p id="id02"></p>
<script>

document.getElementById("id02").innerHTML = document.g
etElementById("id01").nodeName;

</script>
```

Note: nodeName always holds the uppercase tag name of the HTML element.

Property of nodeValue

The nodeValue attribute defines the node's value.

- nodeValue for element nodes is null

- nodeValue for text nodes in the text itself

- nodeValue for feature nodes is the feature value

The nodeType Property

The nodeType property is read-only. It returns the type of node.

Example:

```
<h1 id="id01">My First_Page</h1>
<p id="id02"></p>
<script>

document.getElementById("id02").innerHTML = document.g
etElementById("id01").nodeType;

</script>
```

Add Several Event Handlers to the Same Element

The addEventListener() method lets you to add many events to the same element, without overwriting current events:

Example:

```
element.addEventListener("click", myFunction);
element.addEventListener("click", mySecondFunction);
```

You can add events of dissimilar types to the same element:

Example:

```
element.addEventListener("mouseover", myFunction);
element.addEventListener("click", mySecondFunction);
element.addEventListener("mouseout", myThirdFunction);
```

Add the Event Handler to the Window Object

The addEventListener() function allows you to add event listeners to any HTML DOM object, such as HTML document, HTML elements, the window object, or other event-supporting objects, such as XMLHttpRequest objects.

Example:
   When the user resizes the window, add an event listener that fires:

```
window.addEventListener("resize", function(){
document.getElementById("demo").innerHTML = sometext;
});
```

PASSING PARAMETERS

When passing parameter values, use an "anonymous function" that calls the specified function with the parameters:

Example:
```
element.addEventListener("click", function(){
                        myFunction(p1, p2); });
```

EVENT BUBBLING OR EVENT CAPTURING?

In the HTML DOM, there are two methods for event propagation: bubbling and capturing.

Event propagation is a method of specifying the order of elements when an event happens. If you have a p> element inside a div> element and the user clicks on the p> element, which element's "click" event should be handled first?

The innermost element's event is treated first, followed by the outer-most: the p> element's click event is handled first, followed by the div> element's click event.

The innermost element's event is treated first, followed by the outer-most: the p> element's click event is handled first, followed by the div> element's click event.

The outermost element's event is treated first, followed by the inner-most: the div> element's click event is handled first, followed by the p> element's click event.

With the addEventListener() method you can stipulate the propagation type by using the "useCapture" parameter:

addEventListener(event, function, useCapture);The default value is false or 0, which will use the bubbling propagation, when the value is set to true or 1, the event uses the capturing propagation.

Example:

```
document.getElementById("myP").addEventListener("c
lick", myFunction, true);document.getElementById("myDi
v").addEventListener("click", myFunction, true);The
removeEventListener() process
```

The removeEventListener() method eliminates event handlers that have been involved with the addEventListener() process:

```
Example -element.removeEventListener("mousemove",
                                    myFunction);
```

DIFFERENT APPROACH TO PLACE FORM THE VALIDATION LOGIC

Approach 1: Placing form the validation logic only in server side.

If we place on server-side form validation logic, then the net-work round trips between the client(browser) and the server will be improved if the form page is excluded by the server numerous times.

Approach 2: Placing form authentication logic only on the client-side.

Pros: If we place only the client-side form validation logic (JavaScript), then it decreases the network round trips between client and server as the form validation takes place on the client-side itself without going to the server.

Approach 3: Placing form authentication logic both on the server side and client side.

Pros: Write both client- and server-side authentication logic, so the server-side form validation takes place even though client-side form authentication is not done.

Cons: If client-side form authentication is executed, then it will also perform server-side form authentication, which degrades the performance.

Approach 4: Place form authentication logic both on the server side and client side, but accomplish server-side form authentication logic only when client-side form validation logic is not affected.

Write both client-side and server-side form authentications, but enable server-side form authentications only when client-side form validations are not done. This client(browser) directs a flag to the server, indicating whether client-side form authentications are done or not.

Conclusion: Approach 4 is the best approach or method. Compared to the other approach, Approach 4 does not have a performance issue because the server side will perform only when client-side form authentications are not done.

How we will discuss them here? Our main focus is learning the fourth method. But if you detect it, then to clear the fourth approach and first we have to learn the first, second, and third approaches or methods. The fourth approach is internally used in the first, second, and third approaches or methods. Therefore, we will converse with them one by one, with examples of the web Apps.

```
<body>
<h1 style="text-align:center; color:blue">Election
Commission of India</h1>
<div>
```

```
<form action="checkvoter" method="post">
<table style="background-color: #E4E4E4">
<tr>
<td>Name::</td>
<td><input type="text" name="pname"></td>
</tr>
<tr>
<td>Age::</td>
<td><input type="password" name="page"></td>
</tr>
<tr>
<td><input type="submit" value=" To check Voting
Eligibility"></td>
<td><input type="reset" value="Cancel"></td>
</tr>
</table>
</form>
</div>
</body>
```

Server-Side Form Validation Logic

Now let us see how to develop or create a Java web App with server-side form validation logic. In this App, no need to modify the input.html and web.xml file. Only the servlet components will be modified or altered. Add the following logic in the servlet components before business logic.

```
// get form data or info
name = req.getParameter("pname");
tage = req.getParameter("page");
/* Server side form validation logic:- */
// Validate or Authenticate name
if (name == Null || name.length()==0 || name.equals("
")) {
// " " => empty string
pw.println("<h4 style='color:red'>Person name must
required.</h4>");
return; // stop execution
} else if(name.length() <= 5){
pw.println("<h4 style='color:red'>"+
"Person name must contain minimum 5 Characters.</h4>");
return; // stop execution
}
```

```
// Validate or Authenticate age
if (tage == '/0' || tage.length() == 0 || tage.equa
ls(" ")) {
pw.println("<h4 style='color:red'>Person age is
required.</h4>");
return; // stop execution
} else {
try {
// if age is not numeric throw exception
age = Integer.parseInt(tage);
// check age is valid or not
if (age <= 0 || age >= 125) {
pw.println("<h4 style='color:red'>"+
"Person age must be in between 1 to 125 .</h4>");
return; // stop execution
}
} catch(NumberFormatException nfe) {
pw.println("<h4 style='color:red'>Person age must be
in number.</h4>");
return; // stop execution
}
}
// business logic
// remaining logic
The form validation logic,
// get form data
name = req.getParameter("pname");
tage = req.getParameter("page");
/* Server side form validation logic */
errList = new ArrayList<String>();
// name validation logic
if(name == '/0' || name.length()==0 || name.equals(" ")) {
errList.add("Person name must required");
}else if(name.length() <= 5){
errList.add("Person name must contain minimum 5
Characters.");
}
// age validation logic
if(tage == '/0' || tage.length() == 0 || tage.equals("
")) {
errList.add("Person age is required");
} else {
```

```
try {
age = Integer.parseInt(tage);
// check age is valid or not
if (age <= 0 || age >= 125) {
errList.add("Person age must be between 1 to 125.");
}
} catch(NumberFormatException nfe) {
errList.add("Person age must be numeric value.");
}
}
// display form authentication error messages
if(errList.size() != 0) {
for (String errMsg : errList) {
pw.println("<li><span style='color:red'>" + errMsg +
"</span></li>");
}
return; // stop
}
// business logic
// remaining logic
```

Client-Side Form Validation

Now, we will clear only the client-side form authentication logic for the previous Java web App. HTML5 is also supplying some form authentication rules like essential, min, max, max length, etc.

Form Validation Using HTML5

```
<input type="text" name="pname" required="required"
                         maxlength="20">
<input type="password" name="page" required="required"
                         min="1" max="125">
```

Client-Side Form Validation using HTML for Java Web Apps
Working with HTML supplied form authentication logic has the following restrictions:

- Very few form authentications are available.

- We cannot customize form authentication error messages.

- Writing some authentication logic through JavaScript and some logic through HTML5 does not look good.

We can write JavaScript JS code directly in HTML file as <script> tag before </head> tag, but anyone can see those codes in browser through view page source (Ctrl+U). Therefore, it is not suggested to write JavaScript JS code in the HTML file itself to improve the reusability of JavaScript code across the multiple web pages given by different components, and to hide the JavaScript code source visibility from the browser's view resource choices, it is recommended to place JavaScript codes in a file (generally we use "js" as a file name) and link that file to multiple or several web components.

```
webcontent
|=> input.html
|=> js
|=> validation.js
```

Client-Side Form Validation in Marriage App input
.html Form Page Using JavaScript

- A person's name is needed.

- A person's name must have a minimum of five characters.

- Personage is needed.

- Personage must be the numeric value.

- Personage must be there between 1 to 125.

- Parameter data types and the variable data types will be marked dynamically based on the values that are allocated. No return type is needed for the function but the function can return any value.

The Simple JavaScript JS Codes (validation.js) for the Form Validation

```
function validate(frm) {
// read form data
let name = frm.pname.value;
let age = frm.page.value;
let flag = true;
// client side form validation logic
if(name=="") {
alert("Person name is needed");
frm.pname.focus(); // focus the text box
```

```
flag = false;
} else if(name.length < 5) { // min length
alert("Person name must have a minimum of 5
Characters");
frm.pname.focus(); // focus the text box
flag = false;
}
if(age=="") {
alert("Person age is needed");
frm.page.focus(); // focus the text box
flag = false;
} else if(isNaN(age)) { // must be numeric
alert("Personage is not a number");
frm.page.focus(); // focus the text box
flag = false;
} else if(age<1 || age>125) { // age range
alert("Personage must be in between 1 to 125");
frm.page.focus(); // focus the text box
flag = false;
}
return flag;
// true => form is error free
// false => form validation errors
}
```

In HTML file the JavaScript JS file is used through <script> tag,

```
<head>
<script type="text/javascript" src="js/validation.js">
</script>
</head>
```

In HTML file, the function is termed as:

```
<form action="checkvoter" method="post"
            onsubmit="return validate(this)">
```

Why do we use return statements? When the form is invalid, then we should not perform the business logic, so we display the error message and return it. Then return, it gives control back to the caller method or technique, and implementation will be stopped.

The HTML file (input.html):

```
<!DOCTYPE html>
<html>
<head>
<script type="text/javascript" src="js/validation.js">
</script>
</head>
<body>
<h1 style="text-align: center; color: blue">Election
Commission of India</h1>
<div>
<form action="checkvoter" method="post"
onsubmit="return validate(this)">
<table style="background-color: #E4E4E4">
<tr>
<td>Name::</td>
<td><input type="text" name="pname"></td>
</tr>
<tr>
<td>Age::</td>
<td><input type="password" name="page"></td>
</tr>
<tr>
<td><input type="submit" value=" To Check Voting
Eligibility"></td>
<td><input type="reset" value="Cancel"></td>
</tr>
</table>
</form>
</div>
</body>
</html>
```

See the source code for this App on GitHub. For invalid input, you will get the same result as given in the image.

Simple JavaScript Error Message
In the above App, the error message came into the screen and it blocks the entire form. Therefore, it is not the better technique or approach. We should write a JavaScript JS file such that it should not block the entire screen.

We can use document.getElementById() method or process to display the error message within the same line. It won't block the entire document or code. We can replace the codes of the above validation.js file with the below codes:

```
function validate(frm) {
//read from data
var name = frm.pname.value;

var age = frm.page.value;
// write client side form validation logic
if (name == "") {
document.getElementById("pnameErr").innerHTML =
"Person name is required";
frm.pname.focus();
return false;
}
if (age == "") {
document.getElementById("pageErr").innerHTML =
"Person age is required";
frm.page.focus();
return false;
} else if (isNaN(age)) {
document.getElementById("pageErr").innerHTML =
"Person age must be in numeric value";
frm.page.focus();
return false;
} else {
if (age <= 0 || age > 125) {
document.getElementById("pageErr").innerHTML =
"Person age must be in between 1 to 125";
frm.page.focus();
return false;
}
}
return true;
}
```

In the HTML file, add the span tag with name and age. Use id from the validation.js file.

```
<head>
<script type="text/javascript" src=js/validation.js>
</script>
```

```
</head>
<body>
<div style='text-align: center'>
<h1 style='color: blue'>Election Commission of
                        India</h1>
<form action="checkvoter" method="post"
onsubmit="return validate(this)">
Name: <input type="text" name="pname"><span
style="color: red" id="pnameErr"></span><br><br>
Age: <input type="password" name="page"><span
style="color: red" id="pageErr"></span><br><br>
<input type="submit" value=" To Check Voting
                        eligibility">
<input type="reset" value="Cancel">
</form>
</div>
</body>
```

A problem with the above form the validation.js: After the error or fault message, if we pass the right values, it also displays the previous error or fault message. But it should not display the error or fault message after giving the right input.

JavaScript with getElementById - Form Validation in Java Web Application
To solve the problem, add these lines before or after reading the above form data in the validation.js.

```
document.getElementById("pnameErr").innerHTML="";
document.getElementById("pageErr").innerHTML="";
```

*JavaScript with getElementById Solution - Form
Authentication in Java Web Application*
The Drawback of Writing Form Authentication Logic only on Client Side
The JavaScript codes can be blocked through browser settings, viruses, storms, etc. If JavaScript JS is blocked in the browser, then the user can send the wrong input values. Since the form authentication logic is not written on the server side, therefore, the client-side form authentication logic becomes useless.

To visualize how it works: Disable the JS JavaScript codes in your browser and again run the above web App. How to block JavaScript JS codes in the chrome web browser?

In the Google chrome browser software => Go to the Settings => In "Privacy and security" Section => Site Settings => JavaScript => Block the JavaScript.

In Firefox, type "about:config" in browser's address bar => Click on "Accept the risk and continue" => Type "JavaScript" in the "Search" box => Double-click the "JavaScript.enabled" line to toggle the setting in between "true" and "false" as desired or need.

After disabling or putting off the JavaScript in browser software, if we give the request to the servlet components without entering input, we will get an HTTP status code of 500 error.

When JavaScript is blocked, we should notify the end user with a message saying "JavaScript is blocked in your web browser." For this purpose, the <noscript> tag should be used.

Using the <noscript> tag, we need to pass a guiding message or output to the end user through browser settings if it is disabled or turned off. Place <noscript> tag into the body part of the HTML file. Example of <noscript> tag:

```
<noscript>

<span style="color:red">JavaScript has blocked,
Enable the JavaScript</span>
</noscript>
```

The HTML files after placing the <noscript> tag:

```
<head>
<script type="text/javascript" src=js/validation.js>
</script>
</head>
<body>
<noscript>
<span style="color: red">JavaScript has blocked,
                                    Enable the
JavaScript</span>
</noscript>
<div style='text-align: center'>
<h1 style='color: blue'>Election Commission of
                                    India</h1>
<form action="checkvoter" method="post"
onsubmit="return validate(this)">
```

```
Name: <input type="text" name="pname"><span
style="color: red" id="pnameErr"></span><br>
<br> Age: <input type="password" name="page"><span
style="color: red" id="pageErr"></span><br>
<br> <input type="submit" value="Check Voting
                                eligibility">
<input type="reset" value="Cancel">
</form>
</div>
</body>
```

Now we will get a guiding message displayed to enable JavaScript JS. The below image shows the current output.

JavaScript JS is disabled in the browser - Form validation in Java web app

From Validation Logic in the Client and Server Side

If we associate the previous two approaches or methods, we can achieve this approach where form authentication logic is made available at both the client side and server side.

- **Merits:** If the form validation logic is not accomplished on the client side, it will definitely be executed or run on the server side. Therefore, there is no chance of wrong info or data.

- **Demerits:** If the form is validated at the client side, then it will also be validated on the server side, we are confirming the same logic twice. Let us assume that if the validation logic is of 5,000 lines of codes, then those codes will be implemented or executed twice at different places. So, it is not a good approach or procedure.

Form Validation Logic in Client and Server Side but Validate at the Server Side Only if Client-Side Authentication Not Done

Write client-side and server-side form validations but enable server-side form validations only when client-side form validations are not done. This client(browser) sends the flag to the server representing whether client-side form validations are done or not.

For this purpose, we should use hidden boxes in the HTML form. Using hidden box support, the form page can send a signal to the server or servlet constituent along with the request whether client-side JS JavaScript form validations are implemented or not? If already performed at the client side or user end, then don't perform server-side form validations. In HTML file inside the <form> tag:

```
<form>
<!-- hidden box -->
<input type="hidden" name="vflag" value="no">
</form>
```

In JavaScript file, inside the function,

```
function validate(frm) {
// set vflag value to "yes" indicating
// client side form validations are done
frm.vflag.value = "yes";
// remaining logic
}
```
In the Servlet component or module, read from that data and check the value of flag,
```
// variable
String vstatus = null;
// get client side form validation status
vstatus = req.getParameter("vflag");
if(vstatus.equals("no")) {
/* If client side validations are not done,
 * then only perform server side authentications.
 */
// server side form validation logic
} else {
// when client side form validation are done
age = Integer.parseInt(tage);
}
```

- Form Validation
- JavaScript form validation
- Example of JavaScript authentication
- JavaScript email validation

It is necessary to validate the form submitted by the user because it can have unsuitable values. So, validation is a must to substantiate the user.

JavaScript JS provides the facility to validate the form on the client side, so data processing will be faster than server-side validation. Most web developers prefer JavaScript JS form validation.

Using JavaScript, we can validate name, password, email, date, cell numbers, and other data.

JavaScript Form Validation Example
In the example, we are going to validate the name and password. The name cannot be empty, and the password cannot be less than six characters long.

Here, we are confirming the form on the form submitted. The user will not be sent to the next page unless the values entered are correct.

```
<script>
function validateform(){
var name=document.myform.name.value;
var password=document.myform.password.value;
if (name==null || name==""){
alert("Name can not be blank");
return false;
}else if(password.length<6){
alert("Password must be least 6 characters long.");
return false;
}
}
</script>
<body>
<form name="myform" method="post" action="abc.jsp"
onsubmit="return validateform()" >
Name: <input type="text" name="name"><br/>
Password: <input type="password"
name="password"><br/>
<input type="submit" value="register">
</form>
```

Test It Now

JavaScript Retype Password Authentication

```
<script type="text/javascript">
function matchpass(){
var firstpassword=document.f1.password.value;
var secondpassword=document.f1.password2.value;
if(firstpassword==secondpassword){
return true;
```

```
}
else{
alert("password must be the same!");
return false;
}
}
</script>
<form name="f1" action="register.jsp" onsubmit="return
matchpass()">
Password:<input type="password" name="password"
                                    /><br/>
Re-enter Password:<input type="password"
                                name="password2"/><br/>
<input type="submit">
</form>
```

Test It Now
JavaScript Number Validation
Let us validate the text field for numeric values only. Here, we are using
isNaN() function.

```
<script>
function validate(){
var num=document.myform.num.value;
if (isNaN(num)){
document.getElementById("numloc").innerHTML="Enter the
                                Numeric value only";
return false;
}else{
return true;
}
}
</script>
<form name="myform" onsubmit="return validate()" >
Number: <input type="text" name="num"><span
                    id="numloc"></span><br/>
<input type="submit" value="submit">
</form>
```

Test It Now
JavaScript Validation with Image

Let us see an interactive JavaScript form authentication example that displays correct and incorrect images if the input is correct or incorrect.

```
<script>
function validate(){
var name=document.f1.name.value;
var password=document.f1.password.value;
var status=false;
if(name.length<1){
document.getElementById("nameloc").innerHTML=
" <img src='unchecked.gif'/> Please enter your full
                                    name";
status=false;
}else{
document.getElementById("nameloc").innerHTML=" <img
                    src='checked.gif'/>";
status=true;
}
if(password.length<6){
document.getElementById("passwordloc").innerHTML=
" <img src='unchecked.gif'/> Password must be at
                        least 6 char long";
status=false;
}else{
document.getElementById("passwordloc").innerHTML="
                    <img src='checked.gif'/>";
}
return status;
}
</script>
<form name="f1" action="#" onsubmit="return
validate()">
<table>
<tr><td>Enter Name:</td><td><input type="text"
                                    name="name"/>
<span id="nameloc"></span></td></tr>
<tr><td>Enter Password:</td><td><input
                type="password" name="password"/>
<span id="passwordloc"></span></td></tr>
<tr><td colspan="2"><input type="submit"
                    value="register"/></td></tr>
</table>
</form>
```

Code Explanation

The above complete codes are based on HTML and JavaScript JS.

In the HTML body section, we have formed four input types as the checkboxes and two more input types as a button, and for the input types as a button, we have formed one button for choosing the checkboxes, where onClick (), the selects () function will summon and the other one for rejecting the checkboxes (if selected any/all), where onClick () the deselect () function will summon.

When the user hits the "Select All" button, it navigates to the script sections, where it locates the selects () function and executes the statements contained within it.

Similarly, when the user, after choosing the checkboxes, clicks on the "Deselect All" button, then deselect () function gets appealed. Furthermore, if the user has only selected one or two checkboxes, clicking the "Deselect All" button will deselect those, and if the user has not selected any checkboxes and then selecting the "Deselect All" button, then no action will be presented or performed.

The user can generate many such examples of using the checkboxes and try out such fun.

So, in this way user can select all or discard all checkboxes.

Bibliography

5 Health Benefits of Chicken Wings. (2022, July 7). TheSite.Org. https://www
.thesite.org/health-benefits-of-chicken-wings/

20 JavaScript Interview Questions - Part 2 | Theory and Practice. (2019, March 15).
Soshace. https://soshace.com/30-javascript-interview-questions-part-2/

Abiodun, A. D. (2020, June 24). *A Practical Guide to Testing React Applications
with Jest.* Smashing Magazine. https://www.smashingmagazine.com/2020
/06/practical-guide-testing-react-applications-jest/

Atto, E. (2020, April 20). *Understanding the Fundamentals of Routing in React.*
Medium. https://medium.com/the-andela-way/understanding-the-funda-
mentals-of-routing-in-react-b29f806b157e

Borges, R. (n.d.). *(JAVASCRIPT) - Learning React Functional Web Development
with React and Redux - Algoritmo e Programação - 38.* Passei Direto.
Retrieved July 11, 2022, from https://www.passeidireto.com/arquivo
/107550538/javascript-learning-react-functional-web-development-with
-react-and-redux/38

Catal, M. (2019, October 13). *How to Set Up Lazy Loading Components in
React.* Medium. https://muratcatal.medium.com/lazy-loading-in-react
-2a43ea2b2dd1

Complex State Management with Redux - Pro React - PDF Free Download. (n.d.).
Docobook.Com. Retrieved July 11, 2022, from https://docobook.com/com-
plex-state-management-with-redux-pro-react.html

Conditional Rendering. (n.d.). React. Retrieved July 11, 2022, from https://reactjs
.org/docs/conditional-rendering.html

Context api in React.js. (n.d.). Retrieved July 11, 2022, from https://www.tutorial-
spoint.com/context-api-in-react-js

Dashora, S. (2022, March 24). *How to use React Context with Class Component?*
ProgressiveWebNinja. https://progressivewebninja.com/how-to-use-react
-context-with-class-components/

Entering Multiple Voices with Layers. (n.d.). Retrieved July 11, 2022, from
https://usermanuals.finalemusic.com/FinaleWin/Content/Finale/
Tut2EnteringNotes4.htm

Event Bubbling and Capturing in JavaScript. (n.d.). javatpoint. Retrieved July 11,
2022, from https://www.javatpoint.com/event-bubbling-and-capturing-in
-javascript

Explore Microsoft Dynamics 365 Finance and Operations Together. (2022, June 30). Microsoft Dynamics 365. https://exploredynamics365.home.blog/

facebook. (2022, July 11). *GitHub - Facebook/Flipper: A Desktop Debugging Platform for Mobile Developers.* GitHub. https://github.com/facebook/flipper

fdecampredon. (n.d.). *react-typescript/react.d.ts at master - fdecampredon/react-typescript.* GitHub. Retrieved July 11, 2022, from https://github.com/fde-campredon/react-typescript/blob/master/declarations/react.d.ts

Form Validation in Java Servlet. (2021, May 12). Know Program. https://www.knowprogram.com/servlet/form-validation-in-java-servlet/

Form Validation. (2016, July 4). Gist. https://gist.github.com/ABKC/bafd9c461d671e966552a13a7ce7bdae

Fraser, D. (2018, July 17). *Mocking HTTP Requests with Nock.* Medium. https://codeburst.io/testing-mocking-http-requests-with-nock-480e3f164851

Ghodekar, Y. (2021, February 13). *What is DOM Manipulation? In this Blog, We Will Learn What is DOM....* Medium. https://medium.com/swlh/what-is-dom-manipulation-dd1f701723e3

How to Pass Parameters to a Destination URL Through Tracking Links. (2022, March 11). ClickMeter Blog. https://blog.clickmeter.com/passing-parameters-through-tracking-link/

https://vanvelzermath.weebly.com/uploads/2/3/5/2/23525212/3.4_equivalent_linear_relations.pdf

https://w3cschoool.com/react-introduction

https://w3cschoool.com/tutorial/how-to-select-all-checkboxes-using-javascript

https://www.javatpoint.com/pros-and-cons-of-react

Introduction to Redux Saga. (n.d.). LoginRadius Blog. Retrieved July 11, 2022, from https://www.loginradius.com/blog/engineering/introduction-to-redux-saga/

javascript - How to Resume Script When New Window Loads. (2011, June 17). Stack Overflow. https://stackoverflow.com/questions/6386995/how-to-resume-script-when-new-window-loads

javascript - TypeError: Super Expression Must Be Null or a Function, Not Undefined with Babeljs. (2016, March 3). Stack Overflow. https://stackoverflow.com/questions/35777991/typeerror-super-expression-must-be-null-or-a-function-not-undefined-with-babel

JavaScript DOM EventListener. (n.d.). Retrieved July 11, 2022, from https://www.w3schools.com/JS/js_htmldom_eventlistener.asp

JavaScript Form. (n.d.). javatpoint. Retrieved July 11, 2022, from https://www.javatpoint.com/javascript-form

JavaScript Form Validation. (n.d.). javatpoint. Retrieved July 11, 2022, from https://www.javatpoint.com/javascript-form-validation

JavaScript Form Validation. (n.d.). Retrieved July 11, 2022, from https://www.w3schools.com/JS/js_validation.asp

Jesus Becker Becker « Art Might. (n.d.). Just Art. Retrieved July 11, 2022, from https://artmight.com/user/profile/518482

Kumar, R. (2022, March 17). *What is reactjs and How it works? An Overview and Its Use Cases.* DevOpsSchool.Com. https://www.devopsschool.com/blog/what-is-reactjs-and-how-it-works-an-overview-and-its-use-cases/

Laichenkov, Y. (2022, April 11). *API Testing with Playwright & Odottaa*. Medium. https://elaichenkov.medium.com/api-testing-with-playwright-odottaa-77451917342f

Lazy loading in React. (n.d.). LoginRadius Blog. Retrieved July 11, 2022, from https://www.loginradius.com/blog/engineering/lazy-loading-in-react/

Learning React: Functional Web Development with React and Redux [1ed.] 1491954620, 9781491954621 - DOKUMEN.PUB. (n.d.). Dokumen.Pub. Retrieved July 11, 2022, from https://dokumen.pub/learning-react-functional-web-development-with-react-and-redux-1nbsped-1491954620-9781491954621.html

Maurya, P. (2019, December 14). *How to Import or Use Images in ReactJS*. https://www.tutorialswebsite.com/how-to-import-or-use-images-in-reactjs/

MFC. (n.d.). Getting Started. Retrieved July 11, 2022, from https://www.tutorialspoint.com/mfc/mfc_getting_started.htm

Myntra PPMP. (n.d.). Vinculum Knowledge Central. Retrieved July 11, 2022, from https://vinculumhelpdesk.freshdesk.com/support/solutions/articles/9000198514-myntra-ppmp

The Power of UserDefaults in Swift. (2019, March 3). Swift by Sundell. https://www.swiftbysundell.com/articles/the-power-of-userdefaults-in-swift/

Programmatic Navigation – Navi. (n.d.). Frontend Armory. Retrieved July 11, 2022, from https://frontarm.com/navi/en/guides/programmatic-navigation/

Programmatically Navigate with React Router. (2021, January 12). Telerik Blogs. https://www.telerik.com/blogs/programmatically-navigate-with-react-router

React Book - Router and Query Params. (n.d.). Retrieved July 11, 2022, from https://softchris.github.io/books/react/router-parameters/

React Form Validation. (n.d.). Educative: Interactive Courses for Software Developers. Retrieved July 11, 2022, from https://www.educative.io/answers/react-form-validation

React Render Props解 释_culiu9261的 博 客-CSDN博 客. (2001, June 11). https://blog.csdn.net/culiu9261/article/details/107539020

React Router. (n.d.). javatpoint. Retrieved July 11, 2022, from https://www.javatpoint.com/react-router

React Testing Library – Tutorial with JavaScript Code Examples. (2021, March 7). freeCodeCamp.Org. https://www.freecodecamp.org/news/react-testing-library-tutorial-javascript-example-code/

React.Component. (n.d.). React. Retrieved July 11, 2022, from https://reactjs.org/docs/react-component.html

React.js Render Props. (2021, March 15). GeeksforGeeks. https://www.geeksforgeeks.org/react-js-render-props/

React Enlightenment. (2020, March 28). *8.2 Working with Component State*. https://www.mianshigee.com/tutorial/ReactEnlightenment/react-state-8.2.md

ReactEnlightenment.com. (n.d.). *3.1 Using react.js & react-dom.js*. React Enlightenment [DRAFT]. Retrieved July 11, 2022, from https://reactenlightenment.com/react-basic-setup/3.1.html

ReactEnlightenment.com. (n.d.). *3.2 Using JSX via Babel*. React Enlightenment [DRAFT]. Retrieved July 11, 2022, from https://reactenlightenment.com/react-basic-setup/3.2.html

ReactEnlightenment.com. (n.d.). *7.1 What are Component Props?* React Enlightenment. Retrieved July 11, 2022, from https://www.reactenlightenment.com/react-props/7.1.html

ReactEnlightenment.com. (n.d.). *8.2 Working with Component State*. React Enlightenment. Retrieved July 11, 2022, from https://reactenlightenment.com/react-state/8.2.html

ReactEnlightenment.com. (n.d.). *8.3 State vs. Props*. React Enlightenment [DRAFT]. Retrieved July 11, 2022, from https://reactenlightenment.com/react-state/8.3.html

reactjs - Why is Lazy Loading Not the Default for React? (2019, November 5). Stack Overflow. https://stackoverflow.com/questions/58710241/why-is-lazy-loading-not-the-default-for-react

redux-saga. (n.d.). *redux-saga/BeginnerTutorial.md at Master*. GitHub. Retrieved July 11, 2022, from https://github.com/redux-saga/redux-saga/blob/master/docs/introduction/BeginnerTutorial.md

Render Props. (n.d.). React. Retrieved July 11, 2022, from https://reactjs.org/docs/render-props.html

risalat. (2020, August 3). *How to get Rid of Hair Algae in a Reef Tank: Complete Guide*. Reef Craze. https://reefcraze.com/hair-algae-in-a-reef-tank/

rocLv. (n.d.). *Extracting Container Components Visibletodolist Addtodo*. Retrieved July 11, 2022, from https://roclv.gitbooks.io/redux-getting-started/content/23.redux-extracting-container-components-visibletodolist-addtodo.html

S.M., it19214580 B. (2021, May 31). *React js*. Medium. https://maleeshabulner.medium.com/react-js-5c6420883b6a

Saraf, P. (2020, October 12). *The React Context API. Hello Everyone! Today We Are Going to....* Medium. https://medium.com/cleverprogrammer/the-react-context-api-364da590aa73

Sharma, V., & View My Complete Profile. (2019, June 28). *Microsoft Dynamics AX*. Posting Profiles. https://dynamicsaxsharma.blogspot.com/2019/06/posting-profiles.html

Singh, M. (2021, June 15). *Top 5 React JS Training Institutes in Chandigarh*. Training Institute Mohali. https://traininginmohali.com/chandigarh/top-5-react-js-training-institutes-in-chandigarh/

Sketch Me! (2021, March 19). App Store. https://apps.apple.com/gb/app/sketch-me/id364365478

softchris. (n.d.). *react-book/lazy-loading.md at master - softchris/react-book*. GitHub. Retrieved July 11, 2022, from https://github.com/softchris/react-book/blob/master/4-routing/lazy-loading.md

Start Working with React Context API. (2021, August 11). DEV Community. https://dev.to/pankajkumar/start-working-with-react-context-api-38h

Styling Components in React. (2020, May 14). Smashing Magazine. https://www.smashingmagazine.com/2020/05/styling-components-react/

Taming the React Setup. (2016, May 25). Telerik Blogs. https://www.telerik.com/blogs/taming-react-setup

There's Never been a Better Time to Study Agriculture. (2022, June 20). The University of Sydney. https://www.sydney.edu.au/science/news-and-events/2022/06/20/there-s-never-been-a-better-time-to-study-agriculture.html

Top 65 React Interview Questions (2022). (n.d.). javatpoint. Retrieved July 11, 2022, from https://www.javatpoint.com/react-interview-questions

Working with Styled-components in React. (n.d.). Engineering Education (EngEd) Program | Section. Retrieved July 11, 2022, from https://www.section.io/engineering-education/working-with-styled-components-in-react/

WTF is JSX? (n.d.). Egghead. Retrieved July 11, 2022, from https://egghead.io/learn/react/beginners/wtf-is-jsx

Index

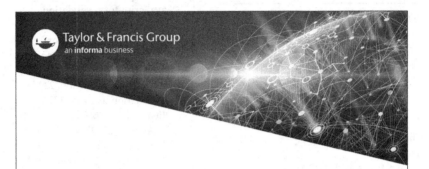

Printed in the United States
by Baker & Taylor Publisher Services